The musician's body:
a maintenance manual for peak performance

Jaume Rosset i Llobet and George Odam

Illustrated by Àxel Oliveres i Gili

Guildhall SCHOOL of Music & Drama

a ASHGATE

Co-published in 2007 by:

The Guildhall School of Music & Drama
Barbican
Silk Street
LONDON
EC2Y 8DT
England
Tel: 0044 (0)207 628 2571
Fax: 0044 (0)207 382 7212
www.gsmd.ac.uk

and

Ashgate Publishing Limited
Gower House
Croft Road
ALDERSHOT
Hants
GU11 3HR
England
Tel: 0044 (0) 1252 331551
Fax: 0044 (0) 1252 344405
www.ashgate.com

Ashgate Publishing Company
Suite 420
101 Cherry Street
Burlington, VT 05401-4405 USA

British Library Cataloguing in Publication Data

Rosset i Llobet, Jaume
  The musician's body : a maintenance manual for peak performance
  1. Music - Performance - Physiological aspects
  2. Practicing (Music) - Physiological aspects 3. Music - Performance - Psychological aspects 4. Practicing (Music) - Psychological aspects
  I. Title II. Odam, George
  781.4'3

  ISBN-13: 9780754662105

Library of Congress Cataloging-in-Publication Data

Rosset i Llobet, Jaume.
  The musician's body : a maintenance manual for peak performance / by Jaume Rosset i Llobet ; edited by George Odam.
       p. cm.
  Includes bibliographical references (p.) and index.
  ISBN 978-0-7546-6210-5 (alk. paper)
  1. Music--Performance--Physiological aspects. 2. Practicing (Music)--Physiological aspects. 3. Music--Performance--Psychological aspects. 4. Practicing (Music)--Psychological aspects. I. Odam, George. II. Title.

  ML3820.R67 2007
  781.4'3--dc22

                              2007002032
  ISBN: 978-0-7546-6210-5

Printed and bound in Great Britain by CPI Bath.

Acknowledgements

Due to the wide range of topics included, this manual would not be possible without the contribution of many people.

We wish specially to thank the following people for their contributions and revisions: Dr Victor Candia, Dr Álvaro Pascual-Leone, Dr Sílvia Nogareda, Dr Pilar Murtró, Sílvia Fàbregas and Dr Eduard Pèrez in the areas of memorisation/learning/psychology, brain functionalism, ergonomics, voice care, posture and dietetics, respectively.

We also want to acknowledge the work of our advisory team of Alice Hughes, Drusilla Redman, Dr Penny Wright, Professor Brian Hurwitz, Dr Christopher Wynn Parry, students of the Guildhall School of Music & Drama (with special thanks to Scott Wilson), staff of ESMUC and Josep Maria Vilar, and staff of the Queensland Conservatorium, Griffiths University, all of whom have read through the first drafts and commented upon each chapter as it has been written.

Contents

In memory of
Àxel Oliveres i Gili

The human body is a miracle of engineering but, like any other machine, it needs careful ownership and regular maintenance. We each of us inhabit our bodies for so long that we can easily take them for granted.

Musicians put enormous strain on various parts of their bodies and this book will help you be alert to things which may go wrong and to how to put them right. Musicians and music students of all ages will find in this book a mine of information about how to get in shape and stay in shape. I hope that you will find the guidance useful and that it will help you to achieve peak performance in your studies and your future career.

Professor Barry Ife CBE FKC HonFRAM
Principal
Guildhall School of Music & Drama

Foreword

GriffithUNIVERSITY
Queensland Conservatorium

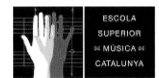

Across the world, young musicians apply themselves to developing and perfecting their skills in performance. This requires enormous concentration and dedication of the mind, but also demands much from the body, whether the instrument is physically located inside, as with voice, or outside, as with most instruments.

We are becoming increasingly aware that balanced and sustainable musicianship depends on a synergy between body, mind and soul. While there is a wealth of publications on technique, repertoire and interpretation for voice and most instruments, there is relatively no literature on healthy modes of playing from a physical perspective.

It is for that reason that I applaud this publication, which we are proud to have contributed to. I express the hope that students all over the globe will gain increased awareness and find concrete benefit from this book.

Professor Peter Roennfeldt
Director
Queensland Conservatorium
Griffith University

The Escola Superior de Música de Catalunya has worked since its foundation to offer musical training that adapts to the professional and social needs of musicians.

Musical activity is not possible without the musician's body being healthy and at an optimum level of response, so we have already included some training in preventive aspects and body work in our curriculum. However, we are aware that it is impossible for such advice to cover the the entire range of significantly relevant information for the musician. It is for this reason that we did not hesitate to become active participants in this international project of creation and evaluation of materials that, undoubtedly, will contribute to this training.

Now the manual is a reality. We believe that the rigour with which it has been created and the intense process of comparison and meticulous revision of the material are guarantee of its suitability. That is why, even though were are aware that the process of evaluation and revision of this material must still continue, we feel happy at having contributed to being able to place it in the hands of our students and of all those in the music schools that so desire it a work tool. We are sure it will have a positive effect on the teaching of music, on the interpretative quality of our musicians and finally, but equally important, on their quality of life.

Salvador Mas Conde
Director
Escola Superior de Música de Catalunya

Being well, playing better

Huib Schippers

Queensland Conservatorium Research Centre, Griffiths University, Brisbane, Australia

Music has the capacity to move us, lift us, inspire us, challenge us, energise us or relax us. People feel to music, think to music, work to music, worship to music, dance to music and even make love to music. It has the power to communicate aspects of the human essence that are intangible, subtle and complex, and it greatly enriches human life.

Making music is an intricate, skilled and demanding activity, way beyond the scope of current scientific analysis. It brings together a baffling array of the best the human mind and body can offer, demanding a well-balanced combination of mental, expressive and physical excellence. This is especially true at the level of professional musicians, who demand peak performance from their minds, hearts and bodies on a daily basis. Although most musicians have been trained well in learning to understand and interpret their chosen repertoire, the physical preparation can often be limited to contact with the instrument. Most teachers insist that their students must practise for many hours a day, and those musicians who teach themselves also impose a similar regime of self-disciplined practice. It is known that if damage is done, it is most likely to happen during extended periods of practice.

Music teachers generally have great passion for and insight into their art, but often they have not been trained to give specific instruction on how exactly to practise in order to get the best results from a physical point of view. The best teachers do try to give general advice to their students, but sometimes without considering sufficiently the precise physiological differences between the musicians in their care. This book can help teachers, their students and practising musicians to understand these problems a little better.

Musicians will generally agree that awareness of one's body and its needs is essential for achieving peak performance, without really doing much about it. But in other fields of performance where the body is also expected to achieve at a high level, such as in sport, things are very different. All sports professionals and many amateurs consult physiotherapists for advice on how to avoid injury, carefully consider and control their diet, and always use warming-up and cooling-down regimes. Sportsmen and – women take the systematic daily training of their bodies very seriously. Musicians, on the other hand, often ignore any such practices and work for long hours in poor conditions without ever considering the long-term damage this may be causing, even though, just as in sport, their body is an essential part of their professional equipment.

Recent research reinforces this fact alarmingly and confirms the number of playing-related injuries and medical conditions is vast in all forms of adult music-making. Even more worrying, perhaps, is how young musicians are affected from the first years of intense learning, sometimes undertaken in early childhood, and recent surveys have confirmed this. In addition, there is a good deal of evidence from conservatoires and music schools across the globe that many students who play instruments that challenge the body – such as piano, flute and strings – disappear from professional training without a trace after reporting playing-related problems. It is also known that a very high proportion of musicians become teachers, often starting their practice at an early age, so the risk of perpetuating physical problems and of long-term damage in their pupils is very high.

Young musicians, their teachers, or music institutions generally do not advertise playing-related injuries as a serious concern. In many people's minds, they are inextricably linked to failure. The idea seems to be that if you are having trouble, you are probably not good enough, so you'd better keep silent about it. There is an unspoken misperception that it is necessary to suffer for the cause of art, to believe in no pain, no gain, and also that it is unprofessional not to work to the limits of endurance. All those who deal with musical health agree that 'no pain, no gain equals no brain'! Physical conditions and injuries have little or nothing to do with musical talent and the chance of making it in the music industry; that is, if they are addressed in a timely and professional manner. If they are not addressed, they will be an insurmountable impediment to musical success: an embarrassment to the institution, a disappointment to the teacher, and a potential tragedy for the young player.

As you work with this book – and that is what we hope that you will do, rather than just read it – notice the way in which it is constructed. We have attempted to analyse things from the musician's point of view. The book is written for all musicians, whether amateur or professional, popular, rock, folk or classical, self-taught, or studying in conservatoires and music schools, and, although we expect that musicians of student age will be our main readers, we hope that the information and advice will also be of benefit to all professional musicians. Most of all we hope that those instrumentalists who teach will read and absorb this information, considering carefully what their role should be in training, helping and advising their students.

This musician's body manual is inspired by the very well-known and respected manuals written for motor-car enthusiasts that are constant and helpful companions to many of those who wish to make their own repairs and undertake successful maintenance. All new machines that we use every day in our homes and at work now come with some kind of an instruction manual and we are increasingly aware of the need to read and take notice of the guidance provided in order to use machines effectively and safely. As in such manuals, each chapter in this book provides basic information under sub-headings with copious illustrations. You will find sections in different colours, with frequently asked questions and their answers (headed 'musicians often ask') in blue and warnings in red.

At the end of each chapter is a quiz. This can be used in several different ways. Obviously it is designed to test your absorption of the information in the preceding chapter. If you get answers wrong, it is advisable to re-read the passages concerned and then try again. The quiz can also be used as a quick refreshment or *aide mémoire* once you have read though the book and answered all the questions correctly. Teachers may find them useful for pinpointing problems for their students or testing their students' knowledge and awareness informally or even formally.

Most musicians will first search through the book looking for references to their own instrument and picking out essential bits of information. This is how we all use books, but it will be very important for all musicians, whatever their instrument, to make every effort to read all the way through the book at least once. Knowing about other instruments will not necessarily be redundant knowledge and should at the very least be of general interest to all performers. Knowing about the musician's body and how it works, even if you do not make your music with that particular part, is essential information for all professionally motivated musician body-owners. The manual has been designed to be read through systematically and sequentially, with the most relevant sections being reread when necessary.

We hope that this book can make a serious contribution to a healthier playing climate for all musicians and that it will encourage and enable them to play in the best sense of the word rather than merely to work. Although it is best used in combination with a proactive course or training programme, even by itself it should create sufficient awareness to begin working towards healthier practice and playing habits, and to be able to react adequately to early signs of playing-related injuries. When these arise, it is of the greatest importance to seek professional help immediately. In the present realities, this help is usually only available outside the institutional walls. Organising this is inconvenient, sometimes embarrassing, but worth the investment.

We live in a world with a wealth of beautiful, profound and challenging music to play, and tens of thousands of talented musicians. It should be a priority of young and mature musicians, teachers and institutions to treasure this rich resource of human excellence, for without live musicians music cannot live.

Brisbane, 2006

Safety instructions

1. Read this instruction manual carefully and in its entirety before using your body as a musician. If you don't do this, it could lead to something going wrong or to less than peak performance.

2. There is no single model for a musician's body. This manual therefore describes the basic parts and functions of a general model and every musician must bear in mind all the possible differences that there may be between their body and the descriptions in the text.

3. The complexity of a musician's body makes it impossible to describe all of its components and all the things it can do in a basic manual. For this same reason the diagrams and sketches do not show all of its parts but only those essential components that help you to understand your body's basic operations. If you require further information please refer to more specific medical textbooks or a health professional.

4. You must remember that, currently, spare parts for a musician's body are not being manufactured and that, in the immediate future, there are no plans for any company to manufacture replacements of similar quality and performance as the original parts. So we wholeheartedly recommend that you try to keep the originals in good order.

5. Not observing the precautionary measures described in this manual leads to more than 75% of musicians' bodies malfunctioning. A third of these breakdowns have a temporary or permanent effect on musicians' ability to perform.

6. Although professional musicians and instrumental teachers have already finished their music education, it is a well-known fact that they have a significant incidence of musculoskeletal problems. The review of the basic functioning of their body given by this manual will be an invaluable addition to their knowledge and a reinforcement of the good practice that is, at last, beginning to take place in the music industry.

Musician's body warranty terms

The manufacturer of your body will not guarantee good functioning, and will not organise replacements or refund what you have paid for your body if you:

- fail to use your body for its normal purpose or fail to follow the function instructions included in this manual (see Chapter 1 – Basic functions, pages 1–23);

- place your body at risk as described in this manual (see Chapter 2 – Situations that place the musician at risk, pages 24–32);

- expose your body to repetitive work in postures for which it was not designed (see Chapter 3 – Posture, pages 33–44);

- use your body with accessories, peripheral equipment and other products of a type, condition and standard other than prescribed by the manufacturer (see Chapter 4 – Musicians, instruments and the workplace, pages 45–61);

- expose your body to excessive volume of sound, incorrect lighting or temperature, or use it in an inadequate workplace (see Chapter 4 – Musicians, instruments and the workplace, pages 45–61);

- fail to take into account its limits and mechanisms for compensating for workloads (see Chapter 5 – The musician's body explained, pages 62–78 and Chapter 6 – Mind and music, pages 79–89);

- fail to maintain your body in accordance with this manual's instructions on proper maintenance (see Chapter 7 – Troubleshooting for musicians, pages 90–109).

Warning

- The instructions in this manual are believed to be not harmful to your body components. However, as not all musicians are exactly alike, you need, as owner of your body, to adapt the instructions in this manual bearing in mind your particular characteristics. This is especially important if you have already detected a defect or if you suspect that you have a problem.

- This manual is not intended as a substitute for the advice from your music teacher or from health professionals, but in addition to it.

- This manual does not have all the information on your body components and functions. For this reason, it is dangerous to try to repair your body by yourself, by following only the instructions from this manual.

- If you experience pain, malfunction or damage that lasts for more than a week, you must seek help from a professional.

Chapter 1

Basic functions

Musicians are very much like athletes because they use their bodies intensively, expressing themselves and communicating through skilled and highly trained movement. Just like a tennis or football player or long-distance runner, as a musical athlete you must prepare your body to deal with the effort of playing and always try to improve your performing ability and quality through effective physical preparation.

An understanding of how your body works can help you to appreciate better how and why it responds in a particular way when you play or sing. This understanding will allow you to optimise your performance and help to prevent health-related problems developing.

The motors of movement

The muscles responsible for producing movement and maintaining body posture are formed by hundreds of elastic threads that are finer than a hair. These are called muscle fibres. Each of these fibres is able to contract when it receives electrical stimuli from the nerves connected to the muscle.

The type of response that occurs depends on how this set of fibres is stimulated. So, in order to pluck a harp or guitar string with your thumb, you need to contract the fibres of your flexor muscles – the more fibres you use, the clearer and louder the sound will be.

On the other hand, if you want your thumb to support the weight of a saxophone, for example, the nerves stimulate only a small proportion of these fibres, first some and then others, to achieve a particular degree of muscle tension that avoids the same fibres always doing the work and becoming fatigued.

However, once the guitar or harp string has been plucked, merely relaxing the flexor muscles does not return the thumb to its starting point. Fibres can only exert a force by shortening – that is, they work by contracting in only one direction, pulling but not pushing the bones. For the thumb to return to its original position to pluck a new string, you must

therefore use muscles that have the opposite (antagonistic) effect to the first muscles. Contracting the antagonistic muscles lengthens the fibres of the thumb's flexor muscles again, returning them to their original position.

Throughout the human body pairs of muscles work across joints so that when one pulls a bone in its direction, the opposing muscle is passively stretched to enable it to move the joint. Learning how to adjust the tension of your muscles in a coordinated way so as to avoid unnecessary muscle work is part of your training. Stretching exercises are a good way of achieving this balance, which is one reason why they are a vital part of the musician's routine (see *Chapter 7 – Troubleshooting for musicians*).

What fuels do your muscles use in order to work?

Your muscles can use two types of fuel. The first is stored in the muscle itself and its composition allows you to use it immediately. The problem is that it is depleted in a few seconds. The other type of fuel is not ready to be used. You have to refine it in the muscle itself before utilising it. A small amount is stored in the muscle itself but, in addition, there are large reserves in other parts of the body, especially in the liver and in fatty tissue. Both the need to refine it before it can be used and the delay involved in transporting fuel from the stores to the muscle via the blood mean that this type of fuel is not immediately available to you.

As a result, if you begin to play intensely without prior preparation you will exhaust all the immediately available reserves before your body has had time to begin to send fuel from the liver or fat. This will diminish your performance and make it more likely that injuries will occur. If you perform warm-up exercises before playing, or begin playing very gently and then gradually increase your work rate, you will enable the energy transfer to 'kick in' and avoid these problems.

It is also important for you to know that muscle oxygen supply depends on blood supply and that your muscles can burn these fuels in two different ways: with or without oxygen. The advantages of burning them in the presence of oxygen are that a much greater quantity of energy is released (up to ten times more) and that residues do not accumulate in the muscle. For this reason, it is better to use this combustion system. However, this is not possible when the intensity of the activity is extremely high or when the muscles are highly tensed (because the muscle fibres themselves compress the flow of blood to the muscles and, therefore, prevent both fuel and oxygen from reaching them). This happens, for example, when the thumb of a guitarist's left hand continually presses too hard on the back of the instrument's neck or when a pianist maintains constant pressure on the forearms while playing. The less tension there is in these muscles, the greater the amount of blood that can reach them, ensuring tiredness will take longer to appear. It has been found that inexperienced electric, classical and flamenco guitarists often use too much force

Although musicians may be very aware of how intensely some of their larger muscles are working, they may be completely unaware of the essential work undertaken by very small muscles.

with the hand on the frets, thereby exposing themselves to unnecessary risk of overuse injury.

If the way that you have to perform music, or the way you hold or play your instrument, does not allow you to relax your muscle groups sufficiently, there is another solution to avoid the early onset of fatigue. This is to relax your muscles intermittently, even if only for a few seconds, to allow the blood to flow around the muscles during these short breaks. Also remember that, for every thirty minutes' playing time, you should stop for at least five minutes and relax, take refreshment, stretch, etc.

Why does the muscle get tired?

The onset of fatigue during a musical performance must be interpreted as the inability of your muscles to maintain the same intensity of effort. Basically, this is a defensive mechanism that attempts to avoid the potential consequences of excessive activity.

In principle, fatigue is reversible. However, if it keeps happening, it may affect the muscles and lead to the onset of chronic muscle fatigue. When activity is very intense or its performance involves large muscles (for example, when playing sport) you can detect if you are overusing these muscles because of the sensations – such as tiredness, tension or soreness – that you feel in them, or through your inability to maintain desired speed or length of practice time. The difficulty is that you do not use big muscles to play an instrument and so these sensations may go unnoticed.

You should remember that the level of effort and, therefore, the ease with which fatigue occurs are determined by three factors:

- the intensity of your performance;
- the speed of your movements;
- and the length of the performance.

These three factors must be balanced to avoid the early onset of fatigue. So, if you play with great intensity or speed, you should do so for a very short time or, in other words, if you want to play for a long time, you should do so with a low level of intensity or speed so that your muscles can tolerate it. The rule of thumb is that the more intensive your practising is in speed or effort, the more you need to take care to give your muscles regular breaks. Because orchestral musicians may have little choice in determining their routines, it is even more important that, when they do practise on their own, they remember this rule and apply it. Such musicians should also make the best of any opportunity to compensate for their lack of control of their orchestral rehearsals by intensifying their warm-ups and by taking every opportunity to use stretching, relaxing and deep breathing during small breaks in the proceedings. For more information see *Chapter 7 – Troubleshooting for musicians*.

There are other causes of fatigue that are also very important, even though they do not directly involve the affected muscle. These can be to do with not paying sufficient attention to the general physical aspects of your body (insufficient sleep, failing to adopt a balanced diet, a sedentary lifestyle, and the existence of concurrent diseases), or they could arise from mental fatigue (overload, stress or interference from other activities). Many students and professional musicians now spend increasing amounts of time working at the computer, so it is very important that you apply the same principles of five-minute breaks in every half hour of work to avoid mental and physical overload.

Ways of avoiding muscle fatigue

Since the symptoms of fatigue will not always be easily detectable, you should concentrate on muscle sensations that may indicate its presence such as tension, stiffness, reduced performance and feeling of tiredness during or after playing. Bear in mind that this may manifest itself hours later, even on the following day, which means that you may not have associated these subtle symptoms with your playing.

If these indicators of tiredness appear, you should adjust the parameters of how hard you are working the muscles (speed, intensity and duration), compensate for muscle loads by exercising the muscles appropriately (*Chapter 7 – Troubleshooting for musicians*) and carefully consider the physical and psychological conditions in which you are working.

As one of the causes of excessive muscle work (and early fatigue) is a lack of control over the effort and tension generated when playing, you must review whether you are using your body in the best possible way (this is best done with the help of your teacher or a physiotherapist specialised in dealing with musicians). Pay attention to feelings of tension in your back muscles, shoulders, arms, hands, neck or face. For instance, check if your shoulders are raised or your fists clenched, or maybe you are tensing your face muscles or jaw. You will certainly discover areas where you are operating with undue tension. Working with certain body techniques such as Alexander, Feldenkrais, Mensendieck, Tai Chi, Pilates and Trager, amongst many others, may be a good way of improving these aspects.

When you are learning a new piece or a new technique or movement, the fact that you are not operating automatically is likely to introduce additional muscle tensions unconsciously. Absorbing the new piece into your automatic system as you learn it by focusing on small components of the music, then putting these together into larger units, will help to avoid such a build-up. Repeatedly reading the piece through is more likely to increase tensions at certain points where the music presents more of a performance challenge. As you get into the learning process, you should work to reduce those unnecessary tensions from the automatic response. If this does not happen and you continue to play the passage with this excessive tension, the automatic movement will incorporate not only the desired movement but also the unnecessary tension.

Similarly, you must train the muscles to relax between notes and to use only the amount of energy that is strictly necessary. You should not consider that you have learned a passage if you have not learned to control the tension between notes.

On the other hand, observe whether you use more force than is really necessary to achieve the desired sound. Once the hammer of the piano key has struck the string, there is no sense in continuing to press down hard. Similarly, the pressure you must apply on a cello string so that the note sounds correctly must be the right amount. After a given point, any additional force will be a waste of energy and a source of tension that will limit or make more difficult other simultaneous movements, and possibly affect the sound. Guitarists should be careful to avoid unnecessary pressure of the fingering hand prior to the plucking of the string.

It would be a good idea to begin to introduce a warm-up before playing and a cool down after playing into your daily routine. You might also benefit from training your muscles to compensate for the imbalances created by playing an instrument and the postures adopted when playing. As well as the customary vocal exercises that prepare the muscles of the mouth, throat and larynx, singers also need to concentrate on the neck, shoulders, trunk and deep abdominal breathing in their warm-up exercises (see also *Chapter 7 – Troubleshooting for musicians*).

Why do you need to train your muscles?

Although the work performed by some areas of your body (especially the shoulders, arms, hands and back) does not appear in many cases to be very intense, it is generally repetitive, prolonged and unbalanced (some areas are worked a lot and others a little). In addition, the difficulty for musicians is that they need the muscles of their hands, arms, face and neck to be able to combine speed of execution with strength. Unfortunately, it is not unusual that a musician's muscles, whether because of muscle make-up or the type of work performed, cannot adapt correctly to the difficult task of being a good speed and distance musical athlete at the same time.

For this reason, as a musician increases her or his demands, muscles can become ever more maladjusted, which may result in chronic muscle fatigue (known as muscle overuse).

By following these guidelines for the balanced working of muscles you can help to prevent problems occurring by adjusting the characteristics of your muscle activity to the demands of performance, thus leading to improved performance. It is most important to pay attention to this if you experience sudden changes of activity level (see *Chapter 2 – Situations that place the musician at risk* and *Chapter 7 – Troubleshooting for musicians*).

Correct training of a muscle, for example in the hand, will stimulate it to create new muscle fibres. It will help to activate those fibres that were not being used, changing the make-up of existing fibres and allowing them to meet the demands of performing better. In this way you can achieve greater reserves of energy within the muscle itself, therefore improving efficiency. Your muscle fibres will be better adapted to the type of work to be performed, increasing blood flow and improving the relaxation of the opposing (antagonistic) muscles during the musical interpretation. Attention to the above considerations will mean you are better equipped to play and also to prevent possible injuries.

The capacity of the majority of your organs increases up to the age of 20–30, but from then on it begins to diminish. Tendons and ligaments lose flexibility from 30 years of age, and muscles begin to deteriorate after 35 years of age, bones after the age of 50.

Moreover, a number of daily activities, including playing an instrument, involve a loss of postural balance and do not involve sufficient energy expenditure to prevent weight gain and the possible development of obesity.

To slow down these changes, compensate for imbalances and improve your physical and psychological state you will find it very helpful to perform muscle rebalancing exercises (see *Chapter 7 – Troubleshooting for musicians*, Rebalancing exercises, page 92) as well as taking part in regular physical activity (see *Chapter 7 – Troubleshooting for musicians*, Complementary physical activity, page 97). A physically active 65-year-old may have the same capacities as a sedentary 40-year-old person.

Warning: Not every type of exercise is equally beneficial for you. Some may even be counterproductive. If you are interested in improving the performance of your body, follow the instructions in *Chapter 7 – Troubleshooting for musicians* and take the advice of a specialist. Do not resort to gyms, uninformed advice or shopping-channel miracle equipment if you are not certain that they will meet your needs as a musician. The most effective regime can be integrated into your daily life, free of charge and without recourse to special aids.

The central computer

Your muscles contract when an electrical stimulus reaches them via the nerves. The characteristics of this stimulus will determine aspects such as the force, speed or duration of the muscle action to be performed, and your brain is responsible for deciding which muscles to stimulate and in what way to achieve the desired purpose.

Let us imagine, for example, that you want to open your instrument case. When you take the decision there is a part of your brain that plans the action unconsciously: it evaluates distances, analyses obstacles, refers to information recorded in the memory (for instance the position and opening mechanism of the locks or how you solved this situation on similar occasions) and studies the position of all of your body parts. Using all this information, it defines the sequence of orders that it will give to your muscles in order to open the case.

During this process you obtain information, both about

1 Planning. When, consciously or unconsciously, you decide what you need to do, your brain, using the sensory information and those memory records related to the task you are planning, will decide which resources you need.

2 Motor orders. Next your brain decides which set of muscles to contract to achieve the required movement, and sends messages along the spinal cord and nerves to activate specific muscles or groups of muscles.

3 Adjustments. To make the various segments of your body involved in an action deploy smoothly, several parts in your brain will be used to initiate and refine the motor commands, precisely regulating the order of the movements and their duration in each segment.

4 Sensory feedback. As well as planning the action, sensory information is used to check and, if necessary, correct its result. If the complete sequence is repeated adequately, you will be able gradually to improve the result and make the sequence of actions more automatic.

external factors and your body, from sensory receptors (touch, sight, muscle tension and joint position sensors, balance, vision, hearing, etc.) that enables you to plan the task with high precision. Even in such simple tasks the body is an amazingly refined instrument.

Moreover, once a chain of movements has been initiated, it will be the same sensors that will inform your brain about how the task is being performed, about whether any changes are taking place or whether any new and relevant information has been detected that you had not noticed. This information will allow your brain to modify the muscle stimuli and achieve precise and satisfactory execution of the task.

These mechanisms function efficiently when the speed is not too quick or when it is not necessary to perform consecutive and complex tasks continually, as happens when playing an instrument. In this case, in order to be able to respond to the difficulty of supervising them, your brain must create automatisms. These are direct paths for completing a task, without the need to monitor all the intermediate stages. One of the many problems faced by classical musicians is that of continuous sight-reading in rehearsal and performance, which may not allow the brain to create all the automatisms necessary for the most efficient action.

Your brain is made up of billions of neurons, which are interconnected. Unlike computer circuits, these connections are not fixed and they may be changed. In fact, they are doing this constantly in an attempt to make the processes controlled by each of the circuits easier.

This operates similarly to the Wonkovator, the amazing lift in *Charlie and the Chocolate Factory*. This machine allows its occupants to move directly from one place to any other in the building, without moving through the intermediate floors or rooms since the Wonkovator connects all rooms in the building. To go to the fourth floor in a conventional lift you have to pass via all the intermediate floors first. The

Wonkovator makes it possible to do this in a much quicker and more efficient way: to go directly to the fourth floor without intermediate stages.

Your brain is able to establish these new connecting pathways and this allows a more efficient response and is the neurological explanation of these automatisms that you need to play or sing.

This mechanism by which some connections are made and not others can be visualised by imagining your brain as a house with hundreds of rooms and doors. Some are normal doors; they connect adjacent rooms. Others are magic doors and connect non-adjacent rooms. The number and characteristics of the rooms and doors is not haphazard, it is determined by your genes. However, as soon as you are born, you begin to use some doors more than others. Each time they are used, they become easier to open. With time it is even possible that those used the most frequently become open corridors without any doors. But those not used become narrower and eventually may start to disappear. Of course, it's always possible to open a new door in the wall, but it is more difficult than using an existing door. And the magic doors – those connecting non-adjacent rooms – are very difficult, perhaps impossible, to create if they were not there beforehand.

Practice does not always make perfect

Playing a musical instrument or singing professionally are two of the most demanding tasks you can impose on your nervous system. They need extensive practice in order to acquire, develop and maintain the technical aspects required to learn a new repertoire and memorise the music.

When you are confronted with a new piece, after analysing and understanding the task, you develop a cognitive representation of it and, guided by your brain, you begin the first movements on the instrument or sound production. Your sensors (hearing, eyes, muscle receptors, etc.) provide information to your brain about the result and, if necessary, you correct it.

Musicians often ask

Sometimes, when I have made significant progress and believe that the task has practically been mastered, suddenly it seems as I have lost everything I have learned and, the more I rehearse, the worse it becomes. What is the reason for this and how can it be avoided? *It is believed that learning a movement is accompanied by a series of corrective mechanisms that provide a set of solutions for unforeseen circumstances. The deterioration is due to a conflict between the different correction mechanisms that are being created. Your brain looks for a way to adapt them to each other or, if this is not possible, creates a new mechanism that is more flexible and more suitable as an automatic mechanism. If the brain is not given enough time to analyse a complex situation and is forced to use two contradictory correction mechanisms at the same time, an unwelcome outcome may result. This happens when you are trying, for example, to learn a complicated passage on the piano, where precision and accuracy cannot coexist with high-speed performance. As a result, movements become inaccurate and blurred although they are quick enough to follow the required rhythm. This 'smudging' is very harmful since, once it has occurred, it is very difficult to eliminate. When this delay in consolidating a movement occurs, you must take a break or make radical changes to the type of rehearsal and exercises you are undertaking, to allow your brain unconsciously to work out a better solution.*

Initially, your fingers move slowly, with fluctuating accuracy and speed, as they are reliant on monitoring the outcome via sight, sound or the feelings in your hands or larynx. As each one of the movements is refined and the overall chain of movements occurs with the desired timing, you can stop concentrating on the mechanical details of performing and focus more on the emotional aspects of the task.

At this stage, we can say that the movement has become automatic and the motor programmes (those magical direct doors) necessary for the task have been created. You have codified in your brain the information that allows the movements to be executed: which muscles to contract, the force you have to use to do this and in what sequence. With continual repetition the programmes will continue to improve, using fewer neurons and making the connection between them easier (with much wider doors).

As you have seen, acquiring skills requires changes in the brain. In fact it is your brain's capacity to reorganise and adapt that allows you to learn and to improve your abilities. But there is a risk that a system capable of reorganising itself with such flexibility may incorporate undesired changes.

Warning: To learn a movement, you must repeat it a sufficient number of times in the same way, with little variation. When the movement has not yet been perfected, the reason for repeating it is to improve it; that is, to change it. If you repeat a movement that is not yet perfected many times without improving the result (which means you are repeating it incorrectly but always in the same way) all you will achieve is to record the information about this erroneous movement in your brain. Therefore, when an exercise fails to achieve the desired results in a reasonable time, you must seek alternatives to prevent the movement becoming automatic in the way it is currently being performed, that is to say, incorrectly. These automated errors may surface unexpectedly in stressful, tense or anxious conditions. Your brain learns a correct movement as easily as an incorrect one and, as a general rule, eliminating or modifying an automated task is usually much more difficult than learning it correctly at the outset.

Memorisation

Another of the basic processes for performing music, in addition to the automation of certain movements and technical gestures, is memorising information that is directly or indirectly related to the piece you are going to play.

There is no single place in your brain that is used to store this kind of information. Instead, the memory is dispersed throughout different areas of the brain. Although the processes involved in memorising are not yet completely understood, acquiring new knowledge, skills or memory is based on chemical changes and the creation of new connections between neurons.

From a general point of view, as with other musical abilities, some musicians have better memories than others – something that is effortless for some people is a real worry for others. Whatever your ability to retain information, it will be helpful for you to understand, albeit in outline, how memory functions and how it can be optimised.

We can simplify the process of memorisation into three stages: acquisition, storage and recovery, and use of musical material. For each of these tasks, you have in your brain different types of memory storage (sensory, working and long-term), adapted to every need.

Stage 1: Acquiring musical information from notation

The process begins when, via one or several of the senses, you perceive information. Let us suppose that you are playing the first three bars of a piece you wish to learn on the piano. The image of the notes on the stave, the sound of the notes you have played and the sensation experienced by the fingers are held for a few seconds in a first store called sensory memory.

The amount of data that can be retained in these deposits is limited not only in terms of time but also in terms of capacity. The storage of new elements in this memory bank eliminates previous data. Furthermore, if the information

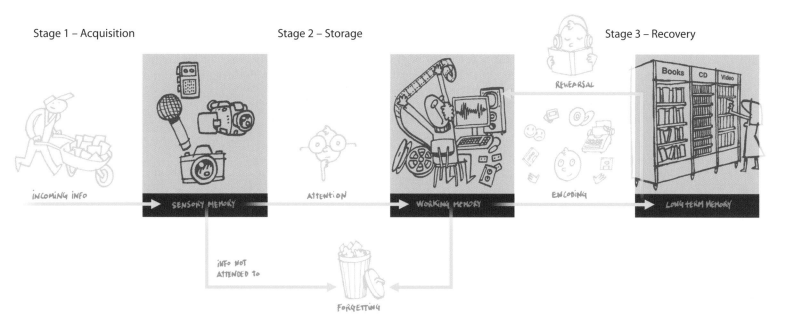

Stage 1 – Acquisition   Stage 2 – Storage   Stage 3 – Recovery

INCOMING INFO — SENSORY MEMORY — ATTENTION — WORKING MEMORY — ENCODING — LONG TERM MEMORY

REHEARSAL

INFO NOT ATTENDED TO — FORGETTING

Books   CD   Video

that reaches the brain from the senses is not clear enough, interference will occur that will make it difficult to retain. So, if the position of the notes on the stave is very similar or if you have played the notes on a keyboard using the sustaining pedal, the sight or sound of the notes may have interfered with the next note producing storage errors. In this acquisition phase, the clearer the information is the more efficient the process of memorisation will be.

Of course, many musicians throughout the world learn without the aid of or need for notation. It may be that such musicians store music with a different efficiency from their note-reading counterparts, but there is, as yet, little scientific study into these differences.

Stage 2: Storage

When you concentrate on information that reaches you through the senses and make the effort to understand it, this data will move to a much more stable substratum of memory: working memory. Information that you have not found to be relevant will not move to this store, which means that a first filtering of the information occurs. If you repeat

a musical phrase two or three times and it is not excessively long, new connections will be established between the neurons of this store and you will be able to repeat it by heart for a few minutes. If it is much longer you may be able to repeat only a few parts (probably the beginning, the end and certain sequences that stood out for you for some reason).

If you do nothing to maintain the neural connections in an active state, the information will gradually fade, especially if, before you consolidate it, you receive new information that interferes with the memory. However, if you repeat it again a couple of times, the retention time may reach up to an hour.

If you repeat the phrase memorised in the recent memory for one day, it will remain in the memory for a week. If you repeat it for a week, it may last for a month and if you continue to repeat it during this period it may be retained for six months or a year.

The more ways you use to codify the musical information (the sound of the notes, their appearance on the stave, their order on the instrument, etc.), the greater the number of associations and connections that will be formed with this information and, therefore, the easier it will be for you to remember it.

Although all musicians must find their own best way of memorising, this is one strategy that may be helpful to you:

1. Choose a segment of only a few bars (no more than seven).

2. Work out the technical requirements.

3. Perform the technical action away from the instrument to avoid dividing your attention between the sound and the movement.

4. Construct a mental image of the technical action by looking at your fingers and, without performing any movement with them, imagine yourself performing it – repeat it slowly three times.

5. Imagine the performance happening without the assistance of the score, closing your eyes to visualise the mental image better without having to struggle against information from the surrounding environment.

6. Choose another segment and follow the same process.

7. When you have completed the process with this segment, return to the first one.

8. If you remember it correctly, go back to the second segment.

9. If you do not remember it, repeat the previous steps until you do.

10. Carry on this way with new segments.

Stage 3: Recovering and using the stored material

Correct repetition of the information will lead to it being stored more permanently in the memory for a long time, even for life. However, you do not have direct access to these stores with the result that, in order for information to be recovered, it has to pass again through the areas where recent memory is stored (long-term memory).

You can remember a piece by how it sounds (aurally), how you feel it in your hands when you are playing (kinesthetically), by the image of the score or the positions of your hands (visually), by its musical structure (analytically) or any combination of these. You should use the method that gives you the best results but try to have a second way of remembering in order to reinforce and facilitate the process.

One way of improving the chances of remembering the piece aurally is by constantly humming the piece to yourself when away from the instrument. If you want to work at it kinesthetically you should play without sound; if visually, you can write it down or draw an image or diagram; analytical remembering can be helped by writing the key points in a notebook and looking at them from time to time.

The way you have recorded information determines how it is subsequently activated and consequently remembered. Thus, data that you have worked on in-depth is much more likely to be remembered than data you have recorded through more superficial effort.

When a piece of information is retrieved successfully from memory, the connections between neurons are made more active and this makes it much easier for it to be remembered subsequently and in a more enduring way. In other words, in order to memorise a passage better it has to be tested repeatedly without the assistance of the score, with the time between repetitions gradually increased. Information that you have not been able to remember should be repeated within a short period of time while information remembered correctly should be repeated at gradually increasing intervals of time.

Forgetting

The loss of, or failure to recall, material previously stored in your memory always has a negative connotation, especially when it is information that took a lot of effort to acquire. However, the mechanism of forgetting is as natural as that of remembering. Forgetting is not only a defence against accumulating data that would eventually saturate your neurological circuits, it is also, above all, a built-in compensation mechanism that helps you, for instance, to erase or mask undesired learned movements on your instrument.

Leaving aside those cases where forgetting is due to an illness or alteration in the brain, the things that you forget do not follow a random process linked to the passage of time, but are to do with an active, specific mechanism controlled by the brain in the same way as the process of memorisation is active and specific.

When we learn to ride a bicycle or drive a car this information is stored permanently in the brain. Musical information, however, is far more complex and so it deteriorates more rapidly. This means that you have to practise memorised pieces regularly to be sure of retaining the information.

> ## Musicians often ask:
> **I feel that I forget the repertoire I have already learned very easily. Is there a strategy to avoid this?** *The principal reasons for forgetting are a lack of concentration during the learning process, poor understanding and analysis of the piece, trying to learn too much at a time, and the absence of review phases. It is a good idea to establish a revision timetable. One plan could be:*
>
> 1. *After an hour of studying (remember that this hour should not be continuous but in blocks of 20–30 minutes with breaks), revisit the material you have learned for 10 minutes.*
>
> 2. *After 24 hours, review the same material again for four minutes.*
>
> 3. *Continue this regular review when possible.*

Strategies to make learning easier

When you are learning something, at the beginning you will observe clear progress but, as the task becomes more consolidated, the changes will be slower. At these times you must try not to fall into repetitive, obsessive and uncontrolled ways of practice. Try to work in the same way as described above, concentrating on the passages which have not yet been completely mastered.

To improve the learning process we advise you to:

1. *Analyse the music* you are going to play before practising it (key, metre, familiar patterns, etc.). This will improve the accuracy of your performance and will reduce the number of physical trials required to achieve technical proficiency.

2. *Distribute your practice.* Learning is better if you work in smaller sessions over time rather than practise in very long sessions. Proficiency developed over a long period of time is retained better than that developed within a short time period. Although longer and more complex tasks require longer practice sessions, relatively short practice sessions are generally more effective than longer practice sessions.

3. *Vary the order of both the pieces and the sections.* If you only practise a piece of music from the beginning to the end each time, there is a risk that the initial parts may be practised in better physical and mental conditions than those at the end of the work.

4. *Plan,* if necessary using a watch, what you are going to practise. This will prevent you practising in an excessively repetitive manner passages that you cannot get right and leaving little time for other sections still remaining at the end of the work session.

5. *Enjoy your practising.* You learn better if what you're doing is 'fun', so find a way of making it enjoyable. Make up 'games' that make the rehearsal more fun and, therefore, more effective. For example, you could aim to repeat a passage ten

times without a single error, increasing the speed slightly each time, or you could play the passage in a variety of different rhythms.

6. *Practise from memory.* The only way to ensure a good performance when playing without a score is to practise without it. However, you should be careful not to 'programme in' mistakes!

7. *Analyse the problems.* Take a very difficult phrase and analyse it. Is it a right-hand or left-hand problem? Is it to do with coordination, the rhythm or fingering? Is it a combination of these? Work at *improving each of the problems separately.* Introduce variations or different exercises to perfect the phrase (for example, accentuate the first note or vary the length of the notes) to avoid repeating a passage that is not coming out right again and again.

8. *Ensure adequate sleep.* The time you spend sleeping consolidates learning as the resting brain assimilates the information it has taken in during your practice, but without any extra information that might interfere with what you have learned. This 'passive' consolidation can even improve your performance.

Mental practice: how to keep learning without your instrument

Performing movements with your instruments or singing 'moulds' your brain to the point where automatic, robust and accurate motor programmes are created. Although many musicians do not consider any learning opportunity other than repetitive practice, you can achieve a similar result mentally without the need to use an instrument.

Mental practice is the imaginary performance of a task in order to learn or improve it without making any kind of physical movement. It has been shown to be effective in improving learning in the fields of both sport and in music. It may be useful to you to undertake when you do not have an instrument, when you are injured or simply when you do not want to overload your body with more hours of playing.

Everyone possesses the ability to improve by mentally practising away from his or her instrument. There is little difference in the effectiveness of mental practice between experienced and novice musicians. Before a concert, Horowitz would practise a piece mentally to prevent his technique being upset by playing on a piano other than his Steinway. Rubinstein found that mental practice was the best way to limit hours spent in front of the piano while maintaining his interpretative skill.

The effectiveness of mental practice lies in the fact that when you practise in this way you are in part using the same structures (the same neuronal connections) as when you actually play. Mental practice can speed up the acquisition of a new motor skill by providing a mental model well adapted to the activity before actually practising it. This not only appears to lead to a marked improvement in the performance but also puts you in an advantageous position to learn skills with minimal instrumental practice.

There are two types of mental practice. One uses the imagination in order to generate positive mental images of oneself performing specific musical tasks in the correct way. The other kind trains you to process and organise efficiently the information that will be transformed into specific instructions from the nerves to the muscles in order to improve coordination. In both cases you can imagine yourself playing internally or externally. Internal imagery takes place when you imagine yourself inside your own body as if you are actually playing or singing. External imagery, which might be used when a person is first learning the skill of imaging, involves mentally watching yourself playing or singing as if watching yourself on a television. Many psychologists believe internal imagery is more effective than external imagery.

Of course, considerable physical practice remains essential.

So musicians should be advised that mental practice should not be used as a complete substitute for physical practice. However, only practising mentally is more effective than not practising at all. Moreover, given the same total number of hours of practice, alternating physical and mental practice results in the same performance gain as physical practice alone. For this reason we advise you to replace 20 minutes of physical practice with 20 of mental practice every day.

Basic advice for practising mentally

Playing mentally is not usually an easy task the first time it is attempted. You should practise it regularly and the training will gradually allow you to achieve better results.
   Mental practice is more effective if:

1. you have prior experience of what you are going to play, either because you know the piece or because you have mastered the techniques necessary to play it;

2. you do it during the first phases of learning the piece, when you are beginning to formulate ideas about it, or during later phases when you are already developing more complex strategies;

3. you combine it with physical practice;

4. the sessions of mental work are brief;

5. simultaneously with your mental image of playing, you also imagine the responses in the muscles that must perform these movements (how the muscles will contract, what feelings it will cause, etc.).

Although if you are interested in studying this activity in depth you should seek more concrete information in textbooks specifically about mental practice, a possible initial approach, for example for a pianist, could be:

1. choose a simple piece;

2. analyse the piece on the stave; understand its structure. Familiarise yourself with all those parts of the piece that do not seem to follow any pattern, study the fingering, imagine the 'story' that the composer wanted to tell with this piece. It is easier to learn something that makes some sense to you than something that does not;

3. look at the stave as if it were a map of the piano, as if every line or space on the stave corresponded to a piano key;

4. begin to imagine each of your fingers on each of the relevant piano keys;

5. when you find it easy, try to start moving the fingers mentally following the score, first with one hand them with the other;

6. if necessary, use a lower performance speed than that indicated by the score and, as you master the movements, increase the speed;

7. when the mental image of the performance is sufficiently stable, try to hear in your head how what you are playing sounds;

8. after performing these exercises for ten minutes or so (or two or three lines on the stave) take a break as this can be very tiring, especially when you are not yet used to it. Try to be systematic and do not move on to the next section until you have completely mastered the previous one;

9. once you have mastered the piece in your head, begin to play it on the piano.

Breathing

Many of us can will remember a friend playing a wind instrument with a completely swollen neck and red face, almost on the point of exploding. If you are one of this group of wind instrumentalists or singers, you should definitely read this section carefully. An understanding of the mechanisms of breathing will allow you to improve your breath control and to achieve greater interpretative ability and quality (as well as ending the suffering of your audience).

Many musicians (especially those who do not play wind instruments) may not be aware of how the way they breathe can be very important for them too. The way we breathe affects our posture, degree of relaxation and the body's ability to function.

We are therefore going to analyse briefly the aspects of breathing that affect all musicians and, after that, those specific to wind instrumentalists and singers.

1. Inhale as deeply as possible. While you breathe out, count out loud as clearly and as quickly as you can. How far can you count up to?	Less than 100.	Around or more than 100.
2. Inhale deeply and observe which part of the body you used to take in the air.	Through the mouth.	Through the nose.
3. Stand in front of a mirror, inhale deeply and observe which area expands the most obviously.	The top part of the thorax, the shoulders or the ribs.	The abdomen.
4. Place one hand on your chest and the other on the abdomen. Inhale and observe which hand moves up first.	The hand on the chest.	The hand on the abdomen.
5. Breathe in deeply again and breathe out in a relaxed manner. Indicate which words offer the best description of how you feel when doing this.	Shortness; difficult; tension; restriction; superficial; laboured.	Fluidity; continuity; relaxation; depth.

General aspects (for all musicians)

The principal function of the lungs is to exchange gases between the air and your blood. When you inhale you fill them with air rich in oxygen – the gas that will be captured by the blood and carried to all the cells in the body so that they can carry out their functions. In turn, the blood will remove the gases expelled by your cells to the air in the lungs so that they are eliminated as you exhale.

In order for this process to take place, the muscles and bones of the thorax operate as bellows forcing the air in and out. The more efficiently you perform this action, the better your body will function.

Although there are many ways of discovering whether you breathe efficiently, the table above offers some practical hints that may help you to find out.

If one or more of your answers is in the first column, you should try to improve your breathing to optimise your performance and relaxation. If most of your answers are in the second column, it is possible that you are already using abdominal breathing, which is much more advisable. In any case, a quick read through the breathing mechanisms may help you to be sure that you are breathing optimally.

Clavicular or high breathing is performed by lifting the shoulders, collar bone and upper ribs. It is not very efficient as it generates tension in the neck muscles, which is bad for you. This is because it involves significant muscle work and also makes it difficult for the blood to return to your heart. Although it is usually due to poor learning, it may also be caused by wearing clothes that compress the abdomen or

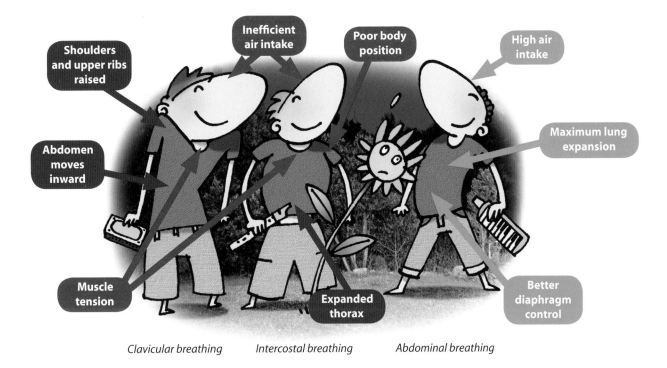

Shoulders and upper ribs raised

Inefficient air intake

Poor body position

High air intake

Abdomen moves inward

Maximum lung expansion

Muscle tension

Expanded thorax

Better diaphragm control

Clavicular breathing   *Intercostal breathing*   *Abdominal breathing*

by adopting a position that is hunched or leaning forwards when playing or performing daily activities (*see Chapter 3 – Posture*).

This type of breathing, although it may be imperceptible, restricts the freedom of your hands to perform subtle movements because of the tension generated in the neck and back, where it may lead to problems. In addition, as the diaphragm cannot descend, it prevents you from inflating the larger lower part of your lungs, which means you do not get your fill of air.

Although intercostal breathing, which is performed by expanding the thorax, allows more air to enter, it involves an unnatural body position and a high degree of tension. It is therefore also to be avoided.

The most natural method, and the one you used as a baby and use when you are asleep, is abdominal breathing. It is the most efficient way of breathing, allows the greatest control and causes the least tension. As a result, it is the one you should try to use when you play or sing or do any other everyday activity.

How to learn to perform abdominal breathing

To recover abdominal breathing you can try the following exercise:

1. Fill and empty your lungs slowly.

2. Force yourself to empty them completely.

3. At the end, concentrate on continuing to push the abdomen inwards in order to expel all the air. Putting your hand on the abdomen could help you to notice it.

4. Keep breathing in and out for while. Do not do it too quickly or you may feel faint due to excessive elimination of gases from the blood.

5. Concentrate only on the final phase of exhaling and pay attention to how the abdomen helps to compress the lungs.

6. Now concentrate on the intake of air. The first thing to move is the abdomen, which moves outwards to allow air to enter into the lungs.

7. Now carry on breathing normally without forcing the exhalation of all of the air and try to ensure that the abdominal movements keep occurring. If you do not achieve this, repeat the previous steps. If you do manage it, try to keep practising these breathing movements to ensure that you incorporate this type of breathing not only in music practice but also in everyday life.

Active breathing
(for singers and wind players)

When your breathing is relaxed, air exits from the lungs without the need for any muscles to work. This is because, as happens when you blow up a balloon, the elasticity of the thorax returns the structures to their initial position expelling the air gently and without additional effort.

However, to control the sound, you must intervene actively during the expulsion phase: firstly, because you require much more air pressure than you get from the simple elasticity of the abdominal tissues; secondly, because to achieve good control of the airflow and pressure you must control the emptying of the lungs with your muscles.

In order to increase the quantity, velocity or pressure of the air expelled by your lungs, relax the diaphragm at the same time as you contract the abdominal muscles. This causes the internal organs within the abdomen to push upwards, compressing the lungs and expelling the air. The more force applied by your abdominal muscles and the more compressed your lungs become, the greater the amount of air is expelled.

In any event, you must learn to achieve abdominal pressure together with the correct muscle control (which singers usually call 'voice support'). If the tone of the abdominal muscles is poor, the pressure will be insufficient and poor sound quality will result. But if it is too high, it will lead to the vocal folds closing or a blockage of the instrument's reed or the lips making it difficult to produce sound and also may provoke a risk of injury.

However, you can achieve greater control of the intake of air if you make the abdominal and diaphragm musculature work in a coordinated way. Although they perform opposite functions (contracting the diaphragm leads to the intake of air into the lungs while contracting the abdominal muscles helps to expel it), if you achieve a good balance between them, one can contribute to the correct action of the other.

These are mechanisms that require a great deal of practice. Additionally, continuously working the mechanisms of abdominal pressure and diaphragmatic counter-pressure will lead to gradually improving your ability to detect, memorise and reproduce the tension exercised at each moment by the muscles concerned. The term 'column of air' is usually used to describe the physical sensations noted in the body when the air has a regular and constant flow towards the vocal folds.

> ## Musicians often ask:
> **When I play very long phrases, I observe that at the end of each phrase the instrument sounds slightly out of tune. I sense that it could be poor control of air pressure but this also occurs on occasions where I can maintain the correct pressure. What is the reason for this?**
>
> *When you hold your breath or exhale for a long period of time, the levels of oxygen in your blood and in the air you expel gradually diminishes and the level of carbon dioxide increases. As happens with variations in air temperature, changes in the concentration of gases within the instrument affect the tuning to a greater or lesser extent, to the point where, at the end of a phrase, changes in the composition of the gases can produce a diminution of up to 15% of a semitone. A trained musician will be able to compensate for this diminution by adjusting their embouchure and breath pressure.*

Producing the voice or sound on a wind instrument involves several mechanisms, some of which are still not completely understood, and requires the simultaneous activation of many parts of your body. As you can see in the table, voice and wind instruments share many of these mechanisms. But there are some differences between them, which make it necessary to provide separate explanations on these points.

Sound production phases			Singer	Woodwind	Brass
	Step 1	Generating the air flow	Lungs	Lungs (+ larynx + lips)	Lungs (+ larynx)
	Step 2	Producing the vibration	Vocal folds	Reed/embouchure-hole	Lips
	Step 3	Controlling the sound	Resonance chambers — Mouth, larynx...	Instrument body	Instrument tubes
			Articulators — Lips, tongue, teeth	Tongue	Tongue

We can simplify the process of producing sound into three steps: the generation of the energy source, production of vibration and control of sound.

Step 1: generating sufficient air flow

To produce sound you must always provide energy of some kind to the instrument or vocal tract. With the guitar this is done by plucking the string with your finger or plectrum. With the piano it is done by pressing a key, which moves the hammer that strikes the string. With the violin you move the bow across the string to make it vibrate, and with a drum you use the stick to strike the membrane.

In singing or making a sound on wind instruments, it is the lungs which, through actively expelling air like a compressor, supply the energy to vibrate the vocal folds, the reed or the lips.

For wind instrumentalists

Wind instruments have other mechanisms that allow you to change air flow, whether to modify the instrument's pitch, tone, loudness or vibrato.

The vocal folds, which are in this case released from their sound production role, can play a significant role in this context by helping to adjust the pressure and speed of the air that is expelled from your lungs. In the same way that you partially block water flowing out of a hosepipe to make it reach further, you open and close the vocal folds to increase the speed of the air. For this reason, some wind instrumentalists take classes with singing teachers to help them to improve control of their breathing and vocal folds.

In the case of the flute, the lips also perform a second level of control of the air flow as they are able to change its direction according to the sound desired.

Step 2: generate the sound (produce the vibration)

The air coming from the lungs is a more or less stable flow. To turn it into sound, you need to transform it into oscillating energy. This is done through the vibration of the vocal folds, reed or lips, which open and close the air flow cyclically causing the column of air in the respiratory tract or inside the instrument to oscillate. This oscillation is transmitted through the air to reach the ears. Here, as can be seen on page 22, you receive the sound vibrations and transform them into electrical nervous impulses in the auditory nerve, which relays stimuli to the brain, which are then perceived as sound.

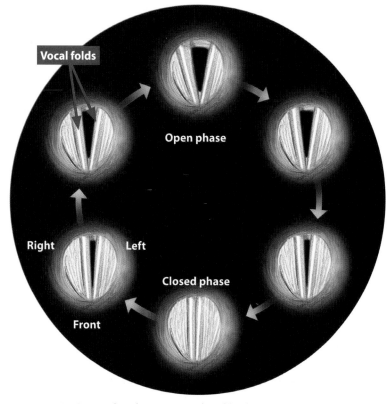

In singers, the vibration is produced by the cyclical opening and closing of the vocal folds

18

For singers

In the case of singers, vibration is generated in the vocal folds (for further information on the anatomy of the larynx, see pages 73 and 75). When you breathe, the folds are completely separated and must be brought together in order to produce a sound.

The process begins when you close the folds and thus the air passage. When your lungs begin pushing the air out, the pressure it exerts below the vocal folds increases. This pressure will push the folds until it overcomes the force holding them closed. They will then open and let the air pass. This will cause the air pressure to return to its initial values, allowing the folds to close again and a new cycle of opening and closing to be initiated. This cycle occurs very quickly, hundreds of times per second.

You will achieve different registers of voice according to the position of the vocal folds, the degree of tension and the action of the muscles involved in achieving the sound. Thus, for example, thick and short folds that make a great deal of

Musicians often ask:
When I am singing I occasionally notice, especially when attacking a certain note, a sound similar to a dull blow that comes from the neck. What is the reason for this? *The sound is produced by the vocal folds as they approach each other – in this case they close too abruptly. You have to try to avoid this by using phonorespiratory coordination exercises (as taught by a singing teacher) since they can become damaged by abrupt closure. On the other hand, if the folds are too relaxed they will allow air to escape between them. This means that some of the air is not used to vibrate the folds and produce a sound but exits the larynx audibly in the form of a breath of air similar to a whisper. The solution for both problems is to achieve the correct degree of tension of the vocal folds through good technique.*

contact will produce a rich and full-bodied sound, which, as the vibration is felt in the chest, is usually called chest register. When the folds are stretched and thin and kept half open and the larynx is in a high position or causing only the anterior part of the folds to vibrate the voice range known as falsetto is produced.

For wind instrumentalists

Wind instruments also have a mechanism that, in a similar manner, interrupts and distorts the current of air to convert the flow from the lungs into oscillating energy or, in other words, sound. This mechanism is usually called the 'reed'. Wind instruments can therefore be classified according to whether they have a 'mechanical reed' (reed woodwinds), a 'free reed' (harmonicas), a 'lip reed' (brass instruments) or an 'air reed' (flutes and recorders).

The reed, whether because it is completely blocking the passage of air or because it is narrowing it, leads to air pressure within the mouth becoming greater than the pressure beyond the reed. As the reed is flexible it will tend to fold or move as a result of this difference in pressure. Opening the air passage will cause the pressure within the mouth to reduce and allow the reed, thanks to its flexibility, to return to its initial position and shape. This process is repeated hundreds of times per second.

With brass instruments, the player's upper lip vibrates with greater amplitude than the lower lip at all frequencies and dynamic levels. As a general rule, the upper lip covers two-thirds of the mouthpiece and the lower lip one-third. In any case, this is highly variable and certainly results in the need for adaptations to suit each musician's anatomical differences (thicker lips, greater muscle strength, differently positioned teeth, and so on).

The flexibility of the structures and the different pressures created as the lips vibrate mean that they do not perform a

1. Pressure in mouth increases.

2. Pressure pushes lips forward and air rushes out.

3. Pressure in the mouth lowers.

4. Tension in the lips pulls them shut.

Brass players create the vibration by cyclically interrupting the current of air with their lips.

simple back-and-forth movement, but that this is combined with an up-and-down movement.

Although the two kinds of movement occur simultaneously, the back-and-forth vibration usually appears mainly in low modes and the up-and-down vibration in high modes.

The amount of lip that vibrates and the amplitude of the vibration are usually very variable. Thus, for example, for the same sound intensity, the amplitude reduces in higher-pitched tones and, because the mouthpiece is smaller, the amount of lip that vibrates on a trumpet, and consequently also the amplitude, is less than on the trombone.

How do you vary the tone and intensity of the sound being made?

When you take a rubber band and stretch it, its increased length results in a reduction of its thickness. The vocal folds or lips can shorten or lengthen themselves at will through the action of the muscles of the larynx and the face respectively. This allows you to change their tension and thickness.

When the vocal folds or lips are not tensed and thick they vibrate at a lower frequency than when they are tensed and thin. A low-frequency vibration results in a deep pitch and a high-frequency one in a high pitch.

You shorten or lengthen the vocal folds basically by changing the position of the cartilages of the larynx through the actions of the muscles in this area (see pages 73 and 75).

In the case of the lips, changes are made by tensing the tissues through the action of the face muscles (see Anatomy on page 72). As these muscles are interconnected, you must work them in a coordinated manner to achieve the correct tension without causing the lip to furrow or its configuration to change, which would modify the characteristics of the vibration and therefore the sound.

While the pitch of each note is determined by the speed with which the vocal folds or lips open and close, the intensity of the sound depends on the extent of their displacement. When you increase the exit pressure of the air the folds or lips vibrate with greater amplitude and produce a more intense sound.

But in order to overcome the greater tension of the folds or lips in high-pitched sounds, you must also increase the air pressure. A novice musician may find it difficult to perform a high *piano* or *crescendo* while maintaining the same note. His or her muscles do not usually have sufficient technique yet to adjust the tension of the folds or lips to the air pressure.

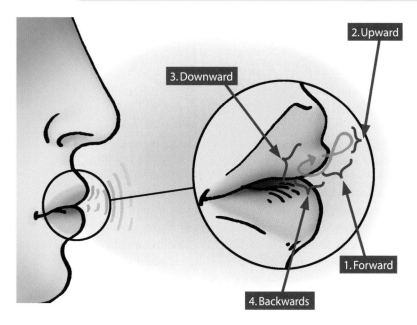

2. Upward

3. Downward

1. Forward

4. Backwards

The flexibility of the different lip structures and the effect of the complex pressure changes produced in that area make the upper lip vibrate in a particular pathway in brass players.

Warning: When you are producing the sound with the lips alone or with the mouthpiece, because of the lack of acoustic response from an instrument, only back-and-forth vibration takes place. This is why exercises of this kind are not sufficient to develop a good lip response. For the same reason, during your warm-up or flexibility work, not only should you perform exercises with the mouthpiece but also exercises that involve a low workload for the lip while working on the instrument.

Step 3: controlling the sound

The sound produced by your vocal folds, reed or lips is raw and complex. Therefore, to make it pleasant, projected and rich, you must filter out certain frequencies, amplify others and give colour to the sound. You achieve this by using resonance chambers.

In the case of wind instruments the principal resonance

chamber is the instrument itself. For the singer, the chambers are the air-filled cavities above the larynx (the upper part of the larynx, the pharynx, the mouth and the nose; see Anatomy on page 73).

According to the shape, volume and characteristics of each cavity or instrument, the air in its interior will vibrate at particular frequencies but not others, performing this role of amplifying and filtering that determines the unique tonal characteristics of each individual or instrument.

Finally, you can adjust the sound through the action of the tongue, lips, cheeks, teeth and palate on the same resonance cavities. This allows you, for example, to articulate sounds such as a 'd' or to play staccato notes on the wind instruments using the tongue, and to reproduce vowels through correct placement of the lips and the tongue.

For singers

In the case of the singer, the sounds produced by the vocal folds have very variable frequencies. To adapt to the entire range of sounds made, it will be very important for you to be able to change rapidly the volume and shape of the resonance cavities. Of all of these, the mouth is the most important since it can adapt with greater ease to the sound produced, thanks to its variable opening, placement of the tongue and role of the lips. Thus, for example, to make a high-pitched sound, you must increase the opening of the mouth, raise the palate as far as possible and flatten the tongue. This makes the cavity larger so the deep harmonics accompanying the basic tone are not lost, producing a high note with a full-bodied and smooth timbre.

Through the action of its muscles, the pharynx (see page 73) can adopt a higher or lower position and thus increase or reduce its volume and resonant capacity. In addition, changes in the larynx or tongue also modify the characteristics of the pharynx. So, for example, when the larynx drops it increases the size of the pharyngeal cavity with the result that the air resonates in this enlarged cavity acquiring a characteristic tone that we might refer to as a fruity or pompous voice.

Finally, there are some fixed resonators whose volume you cannot modify. We are talking about the nose, which is only involved in nasal-type sounds, and the sinuses (small air chambers in the facial bones). Although the sinuses are not able to modify the sound greatly, they can resonate sound internally, especially with high notes. This will give you information about the quality of your voice, leading to the sensation of the voice being felt in the facial mask area.

For wind instrumentalists

The column of air within your instrument vibrates more easily at specific frequencies. Changing the length of the instrument using the valves or holes or lengthening the slide enables you to select the correct resonances for the note you want to play.

Your lips or the reed also have their own frequency of resonance that can be changed by varying muscle tension. However, the instrument resonances are stronger than those of the lips or the reed, which means that the instrument controls the range of vibration of the lips and the reed. This control is not absolute and it is always possible to adjust the pitch of a note by changing the tension. Thus, a trombonist can play a vibrato by moving the slide slightly, while players of other brass instruments do it by 'lipping'.

In addition to adjusting the range of vibration, the instrument, as with the voice, filters out certain frequencies, amplifies others and enriches the sound by converting this 'buzzing' noise into a pleasant and potent sound.

The sound waves generated by the reed or the lips spread both towards the tube of the instrument and towards the bucal cavity (mouth) and your airways. A good part of the energy that moves towards the mouth is lost through absorption by the tissues. However, resonance chambers (especially the mouth and the pharynx) are able to respond to some of the frequencies, as happens with singing. Some skilled players are able to modify these cavities in order to improve the quality and stability of the sound and to assist in a better transition between playing modes.

1 The ear (a) and auditory canal (b) collect sound waves and guide them to the eardrum (c).

As the eardrum (c) is 22 times bigger than the *fenestra ovalis* (e) the sound is amplified 5 dB.

The little muscles between bones (d) can reduce or increase the amount of vibration transmitted to inner ear. This is a regulating-protective mechanism.

6 As the 'hairs' of the cells move, they produce electrical impulses. The auditory cells connected to the auditory nerve (g) finally transmit the information to the brain.

7 The brain decodes the electrical signals and gives meaning to the sound heard.

5 Vibrations reaching the *fenestra ovalis* (e) are transmitted to the fluid contained in the cochlea (f) that, in turn, moves the 'hairs' contained in the cochlea.

2 The sound waves cause the eardrum (c) to vibrate.

3 The vibration of the eardrum (c) vibrates the three tiny bones (d) of the middle ear.

4 The mechanical vibration of the bones (d) produces the oscillation of the *fenestra ovalis* (e).

How we hear

Quiz

1. **Music-making must be considered a highly demanding physical activity. This is:**
   a) true, although only a reduced area of your body is working;
   b) true, but only for those musicians with poor technique;
   c) false, because movements are light, varied, in healthy postures and without tensions.

2. **Talking about muscle functionalism, it is true that:**
   a) all muscle fibres can shorten and lengthen when receiving the correct order from the brain;
   b) each muscle contains two kind of fibres: the first kind are specialised in shortening and the second in lengthening to bring the muscle to its starting position again;
   c) muscles only can shorten and, to return them to their initial position, muscles that have the opposite effect must contract.

3. **Muscle blood supply is necessary because:**
   a) it allows you to burn the muscle fuels with oxygen and a greater quantity of energy is released;
   b) it allows you to clear waste products produced by muscular work;
   c) the two prior sentences are correct.

4. **To undergo middle- and long-duration muscle work, main energy stores:**
   a) are inside the muscle, so you can dispose of them when you want;
   b) are mainly in the liver and in fatty tissue, so some warm-up time is needed to make them available;
   c) could be produced by the muscle, if you have a good technique and if you play or sing in a relaxed manner.

5. **In which of the following situations will your muscles not freely dispose of oxygen from blood and, therefore, produce fatigue or muscular problems more easily:**
   a) when you perform slow musical passages, continuously maintaining tension in your muscles to ensure maximum precision;
   b) when you perform quick musical passages for some minutes;
   c) when you play or sing for two hours, having short breaks for muscle relaxation.

6. As you practise a technique or a musical passage, your neurons:
   a) get bigger and stronger to allow better and more speedy nerve conduction;
   b) reinforce existing connections between them and establish new pathways to make the nerve conduction more efficient;
   c) create elevators with magic doors as happens in famous books and films.

7. To improve or correct a movement you must repeat the exercise:
   a) enough times in the same way;
   b) in the same way but only if the result improves;
   c) until it works.

8. Which of the following practice routines is a good strategy to improve memorisation:
   a) practise from memory;
   b) work in a long practice session;
   c) do not sleep just after practising.

9. Mental practice is a good tool for musicians but:
   a) not everybody possesses the ability to perform mentally;
   b) it is only effective in professional musicians;
   c) it needs to be practised regularly to achieve good results.

10. The way we breathe is important for wind instrument players and singers but also for other musicians because:
    a) the collar bone and ribs need to remove the expelled gases in all musicians;
    b) how you breathe affects your posture, degree of relaxation and the body's ability to function;
    c) there is a risk of neck or face explosion if you do not breathe efficiently.

11. In wind instrumentalists, the vocal folds:
    a) generally do not have any important role during sound production;
    b) help to adjust the pressure and speed of the air;
    c) vibrate to assist sound production

Question	Correct answer	If your answer is wrong, please read the page again and find out why you made your mistake
1	a	see page 1
2	c	see page 1
3	c	see page 2
4	b	see page 2
5	a	see page 3
6	b	see page 7
7	b	see page 8
8	a	see page 10
9	c	see page 12
10	b	see page 14
11	b	see page 17

Chapter 2

Situations that place the musician **at risk**

As a musician, you need to be aware that your body is exposed to factors and situations that could weaken you and cause damage if you do not take them into account. You should try to avoid such situations or, if this is not possible, compensate for their effects to guarantee that you operate efficiently and achieve maximum performance. In this chapter, we discuss ten problems common amongst musicians

Problem 1

Taking more care of your musical instrument than of your own body

Musicians' bodies are trained to adjust to huge workloads, but only if we respect certain limits. If we set ourselves a very intensive work rate, it must be for a short period only. However, the process of learning and practising music is essentially based on repetition – so although the workload could be light, you almost always end up exceeding, albeit imperceptibly, the body's limits of adaptation and tolerance. It is even more important to be aware of this if abrupt changes in the rhythm and intensity of work occur (for example a sudden increase in rehearsal hours, or a change of teacher, repertoire, technique or in the instrument's characteristics). If your instrument was broken you would not play it until it was repaired, so if you experience pain, stop playing and seek professional advice. 'No pain, no gain' is a maxim often heard, but now musicians must be advised that 'no pain, no gain' means no brain!

What you should do

Your body deserves and needs at least the same level of care that you give to your instrument. You should bear in mind that playing a musical instrument or singing are physical demands that must be taken seriously. The basic tools are appropriate physical work, organising and monitoring your work rhythm, planning any major changes (for example, increasing the time of practice progressively by a maximum of 30 minutes every 3 days), caring for your health in both body and mind (see *Chapter 6 – Mind and music* and *Chapter 7 – Troubleshooting for musicians*) and respecting postural and ergonomic matters (see *Chapter 3 – Posture* and *Chapter 4 – Musicians, instruments and the workplace*). Students should understand that ultimately their bodies are more important than examinations, which can be deferred if necessary.

What you should do

You should work those parts of the body that you exercise least, for instance carrying out compensatory physical activity (see *Chapter 7 – Troubleshooting for musicians*), and make certain that your posture or ways of holding your instrument are not contributing to or generating greater imbalances than absolutely necessary, even considering specially adapted instruments (*Chapter 3 – Posture* and *Chapter 4 – Musicians, instruments and the workplace*).

Problem 3

The technique you use

There are techniques that may be musically effective but, at the same time, medically defective. These can become the source of future problems.

One of the principal faults is poor control of tension and effort. For example, a double bass player could play a movement *forte*, moving the bow with greater energy – and simultaneously increasing the force applied with the left arm by an equal amount – far more than is strictly necessary to

Problem 2

Not compensating for asymmetric work

No musician works in a completely balanced manner. The oboist, for example, supports the instrument's weight on the front part of her or his body, creating more work for the back muscles. The right arm of the trombonist moves constantly forwards and backwards but never up and down. Such imbalances can adversely affect your muscles, tendons, joints and spinal column, making you less efficient in your work, causing aches and pains and muscle fatigue, and increasing the possibilities of malfunction and the potential for more serious injury or disease in the future.

Can Seriously Harm Your Health

guarantee the correct vibration of the string. Similarly, some pianists continue to apply pressure, despite having reached the bottom of the key.

Sometimes musicians can put themselves at risk simply through a poor choice of repertoire. Certain compositions are highly demanding physically and may not be well matched to the performer's body shape and characteristics. Musicians who undertake such tasks must always compensate for this by taking extra precautions, such as more specific stretching, taking more breaks and taking longer to warm up and cool down.

The basic problem lies in the fact that no technique can be considered as universally correct. There is no reason why a technique that provides good results for a teacher should be completely suited to his or her pupils.

What you should do

Analyse your natural advantages and also your limitations and discuss these candidly with your teacher. With the help of your teacher, you should choose the technique and repertoire most suitable for your technical, physical and psychological abilities.

Use your energy to play with and not fight against your instrument. Work on your relaxation (*Chapter 6 – Mind and music*) so as to achieve the very best economy of effort and movement.

Problem 4

Unsuitable fit between the body and instrument

The process for designing musical instruments has rarely taken into account the need for a better fit with the musician's body. Instead, the musician must assume an additional load in adapting him- or herself to the instrument.

Often, musicians complicate the situation for themselves: perhaps, for example, by choosing a viola that is too big for the body that will be playing it, or by tuning the instrument to a higher pitch to achieve a better sound. Other examples include the singer who, in order to fit in with the needs of her or his choir, sings outside their own *tessitura*, or the purist attitude of a violin teacher who prevents a pupil with a particularly long neck from using a rest or rib that would stop her or him from having to raise their shoulder or twist the neck excessively.

Unfortunately, the majority of musicians unintentionally adopt unhealthy postures, and the instrument can act as a mask, making a poor posture appear more aesthetically pleasing.

What you should do

If you really feel that the way your instrument fits your body is too uncomfortable, consider asking your instrument maker to modify your instrument, or look for accessories that might help with this. Do not wait until you get an injury before starting to experiment in this area (*Chapter 4 – Musicians, instruments and the workplace*).

A very good test, to be performed with a partner, is to take your instrument and stand in front of a mirror. Close your eyes and play a passage of music. When you stop playing, and without changing your posture, ask your partner to take your instrument from you. Open your eyes and observe your posture in the mirror. Notice the difference between this 'frozen' posture and your normal posture. You may well be surprised (*Chapter 3 – Posture*). Even very small deviations from your natural posture can, over the years, become sources of problems if you do not compensate as necessary. If your partner is an instrumentalist, it would be a good idea to encourage them to try the same experiment.

Problem 5

Failing to consider your overall state of health

We know that playing or singing is very physically and psychologically demanding, and you obviously should not rehearse or perform when you are not correctly prepared. So, for instance, you should not work when you are injured, over-tired, ill, sleepy, have not drunk enough fluids or following heavy meals and fizzy drinks, which make abdominal breathing difficult.

Sometimes the cure is worse than the illness. It is obvious that you must in no circumstances play in discomfort or pain. But, if your finger hurts when you play and you take a painkiller, as well as relieving the symptoms you are removing the alarm signal telling you that something is wrong. Similarly, an allergy may cause the formation of excessive mucous, which is very inconvenient for wind

instrumentalists and singers, but the medicines to treat it may cause the voice to deteriorate and the mucous lining to dry out. Aspirin may relieve pain and inflammation of the throat but it can encourage bleeding of the vocal folds. Some treatments may even lead to irreversible changes in the voice.

What you should do

Use your common sense when you are not feeling on top form. If possible, miss a rehearsal – if you are suffering from an infection, for example. This will spare you problems and you will avoid exposing your colleagues to your germs. You should always seek the advice of an arts medicine specialist about whether treatment is necessary and about the risks before using it. Students may be able to access such specialist advice through their student health advisor. Professional musicians can contact their national associations directly (see the list on p.112-3).

Problem 6

Poor environmental conditions

Often the musician is not conscious of the effect of environmental conditions such as temperature, humidity or acoustics on his or her performance and health. For example, excessive cold makes subtle movements of the fingers difficult, heating and air conditioning dry singers' and wind instrumentalists' mucous membranes and performing or rehearsing in the open air – in venues that are noisy or have poor acoustics that do not allow you to hear the sound you make correctly – may cause you to play or sing more loudly than usual.

What you should do

Try, if possible, to check and improve your environmental conditions (see *Chapter 4 – Musicians, instruments and the workplace*) and, if it is not possible, step up all the preventative measures explained in this manual.

Problem 7

Carrying and holding an instrument

Instruments are not always carried or held correctly, whether because of their size (for example, the double bass or the drum set) or shape (for example, the lute or theorbo), or because of a lack of awareness on the part the musician.

Although it may seem insignificant to you at the time, carrying a clarinet for half an hour by gripping the case handle with your hand, can involve an increased load on the forearm muscles that is greater than several hours of instrument practice.

What you should do

You must think about distributing the weight as symmetrically as possible. Use wide straps, avoid loading the delicate muscles of the hands wherever possible, preferably use the more powerful back muscles and, if it is not possible to carry the load in an evenly distributed fashion, frequently switch sides or the hand carrying the case (see *Chapter 3 – Posture*).

Other daily activities

It is true that it is difficult to conclude that a pain in your thumb is because you have been writing text messages on your mobile phone for 20 minutes, if you have also just spent 5 hours rehearsing with double beaters on the vibraphone. However, be aware of how you use your mobile phone. Don't forget to analyse how your computer is positioned at home, what type of pillow you use, how tightly you hold the handset when speaking on the phone, how many hours you may spend writing at exam time, how you make the bed or do the vacuuming, how you pick up and hold your child or how you use your voice differently when teaching, lecturing or speaking in public – in fact, all the activities you carry out in your daily life.

What you should do

As you read this manual think about the positions and activities that you regularly carry out during your normal daily routine. Think about the load on your body that is generated by these activities and decide if you should change the way you do them or even stop some of them (see *Chapter 4 – Musicians, instruments and the workplace*).

Psychological aspects

Although perfectionism, perseverance, sensitivity and introspection may be valuable qualities in a musician, taken to the extreme they may represent a physical risk.

In addition to the individual character of each musician, your state of mind, degree of nervousness when going on stage, and personal, family or even work problems will all affect your ability to play and your tolerance of workloads.

If you are carrying such heavy non-musical extra burdens, in addition to risking a less-than-perfect musical outcome, you will be far more susceptible to injuries.

What you should do

Besides working on the psychological aspects of your playing (see *Chapter 6 – Mind and Music*) and, if necessary, seeking the advice of a professional, you should pay special attention to practical aspects that can help you to counteract situations of greater stress (things like warming-up, positioning or ergonomic considerations).

In addition, if you have a physical problem, this will probably affect you psychologically. If so, the solution to your physical problem must encompass both areas.

If something doesn't work on your instrument, don't obsessively repeat it to try to force yourself to achieve better results. Change the way you do it; find alternatives; practise it in small sections; be creative. Repetition of a bad movement could lead you to learn it incorrectly.

There is a great deal of research taking place at the moment on performance anxiety or stage fright. This can be treated in many ways, both pharmaceutically and through a variety of other therapies (see *Chapter 6 – Mind and music*). If this is a problem for you, discuss this with your teacher first, who may be able to advise you, but be aware that some of the treatments are quite new and that your teacher may not be familiar with them. In the period just before an important performance – because of your preoccupation with more immediate problems – it is quite likely that you will give less attention to your body's needs instead of being more aware of them. Be aware of this possibility and take appropriate action.

Problem 10

Socioeconomic factors

Many musicians today, especially students, continue to live in very poor social and working conditions. If a professional musician misses a rehearsal and admits that it was because of some discomfort with, for instance, her or his forearm, they risk not being called for the next concert. This insecurity in economic and work terms may be compounded by the fact that some physicians do not understand or are not very sympathetic to the physical problems of a working musician. They may instruct her or him to stop playing, and the musician, fearing this recommendation, often seeks her or his own solutions (such as eliminating certain technical movements from the repertoire, taking extra rest days, self-medication or putting up with playing through discomfort) leading to the medical problem being hidden.

What you should do

Obviously, satisfactory economic and social support (a guarantee of retained employment, economic assistance during periods when you are signed off from work, recognition of the professional illnesses of the musician, understanding and efficiency by the medical profession, and so forth) will make things much easier. It is important that all young musicians should take these things seriously and be prepared to give time, and work together with their colleagues, to achieve better working conditions for all musicians.

Many musicians nowadays are self-employed and take on a variety of different activities. In fact, this may be very advantageous to you, since it provides a good variety of physical and mental stimuli, but you must be careful to watch the balance of your activities and to assess the physical and mental demands these make on you. Be prepared to change the balance if your health begins to suffer and do not ignore early warning signs. Self-employed musicians are also

encouraged, early in their career, to consider taking sensible insurance for themselves as well as for their instruments, considering carefully their probable needs in later life and opting into appropriate pension schemes.

If you fear that your family doctor does not understand performing arts medicine, then seek specialist advice through the organisations that exist in your country (see the list on pp. 112–13). While stopping playing may be one part of the solution, the physician may consider many other strategies. Whatever the case, failing to seek a solution to an injury or problem that lasts more than a week is always a risk, since the longer the problem takes to develop, the more likely it is that treatment will take an equally long time, or even, in the worst-case scenario, that damage is irreversible.

Are you at risk?

Do you usually play for several hours without a break?	No	Yes	Yes, definitely
Following a few days without playing do you pick up your activity gradually, and go all the more slowly after a long break?	No	Yes	Definitely not
Do you perform stretching exercises before and after playing and do you save the more difficult pieces for the middle of the rehearsal time?	No	Yes	Definitely not
Do you play even though you're tired or feel some discomfort?	No	Yes	Yes, definitely
Do you habitually play in the forte range?	No	Yes	Yes, definitely
Do you play an instrument that is heavy, large or has very taut strings?	No	Yes	Yes, definitely
Do you perform physical exercise more than once a week?	No	Yes	Definitely not
Do you sleep for less than eight hours a day?	No	Yes	Yes, definitely
Are you a perfectionist?	No	Yes	Yes, definitely
Do you find it difficult to say 'no' to a musical project?	No	Yes	Yes, definitely
Are you usually under a lot of pressure?	No	Yes	Yes, definitely
Do you choose your repertoire with regard to your physical, technical and psychological abilities?	No	Yes	Definitely not
Do you regularly review your posture in front of a mirror or through being filmed?	No	Yes	Definitely not

If you have ticked the last column several times, consider your situation seriously or you will be booking an appointment to see a medical expert before too long.

Quiz

1. Although all these are risk factors for musicians' health, the most easily tolerated by a musician's body are:
   a) abrupt changes in the work rhythm;
   b) quick increases of work time;
   c) intensive work rate.

2. The physical demands of playing or singing should be compensated by:
   a) avoiding any sport or physical activity outside playing and singing;
   b) organising and planning your work and major changes in your life;
   c) ignoring your physical and psychological problems.

3. Using your body asymmetrically when playing:
   a) is only found in wind and string players;
   b) rarely affects the spinal column;
   c) must always be compensated by appropriate physical and postural work.

4. Which of the following statements on defective technique is false?
   a) poor control of tension and effort is one of the principal faults in all musicians;
   b) even though you have a good technique, some repertoires may not be best suited to your level of ability or your physical attributes;
   c) trying to use exactly the same technique as your teacher is the best way to avoid physical problems.

5. A musician's health and performance are best enhanced by:
   a) understanding that your instrument could lead you to adopt an unhealthy posture and so checking it;
   b) sacrificing good posture and ergonomics in order to achieve a better sound;
   c) accepting that instruments are traditionally designed in the best way and thus trying to adapt our body and posture to them, since accessories and ergonomic aids are only for unskilled or unhealthy musicians.

6. It's not true that:
   a) any physical or psychological trouble can affect your performance and therefore increase your risk of damage;
   b) the way that you carry your instrument is only important if it is heavy;
   c) everyday activities can add important extra loads to your body and affect your capabilities to play or sing efficiently.

7. If you have a health problem you should:
   a) seek professional advice within a year;
   b) not worry – this is a common musician's condition and time will solve it;
   c) check out what could be wrong and what could be causing the problem; if it does not resolve in a few days, seek professional help as soon as possible.

Question	Correct answer	If your answer is wrong, please read the page again and find out why you made your mistake
1	c	see page 24
2	b	see page 24
3	c	see page 25
4	c	see page 26
5	a	see page 27
6	b	see page 28
7	c	see page 31

Chapter 3

Posture
Your body in harmony with your instrument

Few of us will have come through childhood without receiving advice on our posture from adults. They may have commented on and perhaps criticised the way that we stand, sit, walk and play our instruments. We can feel quite self-protective and sensitive about this, since our posture is an essential part of our identity. In adolescence, we often express our new feelings and abilities through exaggerated adaptations of our posture, and our bodies are usually flexible enough at that age for it not to matter too much to us. But in adult life this deep-rooted sensitivity can work against us and as performing musicians we always need to be aware that our body is our business. Finding your optimal posture is a matter of exploration for each individual and we need to acknowledge that how we feel is often different from the reality of how we actually are. This is why advice from teachers and others can be very helpful and also why we need to check our posture, using the guidelines set out here, in as objective a way as possible. A full-length mirror can be an important aid. Postural harmony is achieved through good balance and this will be a key principle.

You may feel quite comfortable and at home with the way you stand, sit, walk and play, and may experience feelings of resentment if your teacher criticises your posture and asks you to make changes in something that, to you, appears natural and comfortable. But feeling comfortable does not necessarily mean that your posture is the best one for you. The posture that works well enough for you when you are younger may be the source of increasing problems later in life. Each instrument presents the performer with a specific set of problems, and we cannot here attempt to describe each one, since achieving the harmony between instrument and performer is an individual matter and needs the advice of experts.

You may find that you need to make some changes in your posture. Changes in things that have already become habitual have to be done slowly and you may well feel less comfortable during the period of change. It takes a while, sometimes months at a time, for muscles to adapt and for a new postural position to become automatic and habitual. Until this process happens you may feel some discomfort or fatigue and this is when you have to learn to persevere and be patient and not be put off by it.

What is a good posture?

Your most effective posture is individual to you and will be achieved when you can balance your body weight well. This makes it easier for the muscles to support the weight of each of your body's parts, avoid unnecessary overloads and perform well for you. Of course, different instruments require specific playing postures, but there are some general principles that apply whether or not you are functioning as a musician. Whatever life requires you to do, you need to learn to avoid subjecting your body to undue effort and stress, risking injury that could threaten your continuing ability to perform.

Let's look at the three basic principles: they are verticality, stability and muscle/joint balance.

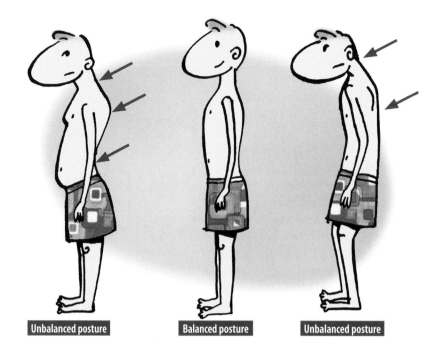

Arrows show over-stressed areas

| Unbalanced posture | Balanced posture | Unbalanced posture |

Verticality

Stand or sit in front of a mirror and try to imagine a vertical line passing through the centre of your body starting downwards from your nose and passing through the chin, sternum, navel and pubis and between the knees and ankles. Also imagine two other lines from each ear, dropping through your shoulder and hip and to your ankle if you are standing (see figure on page 37). Remember the principle of balance and look for symmetry. You could even draw the lines on the mirror or, even better, get someone else to check the verticality for you. While your spine seen from the front should be vertically straight, seen from the side it has natural curves that are essential to your balance and posture (see *Chapter 5 – The Musician's body explained*). However, if these curves become exaggerated this can overload muscles and cause tension and pain. Check the position of your shoulders and also look at how you hold your head. If you are a musician who has to spend a lot of time on your feet try to rest each foot in turn by resting it on a raised surface (about 4–6 inches or 10–15 cm high). This will reduce the low back curve and helps to avoid excessive spinal arching. Achieving a good, symmetrical vertical balance will reduce the amount of energy you need and increase your feeling of harmony. Very small adjustments can be very significant in the long term but the discipline to make and maintain these small changes needs constant checking and thought.

Stability

To have and maintain a good posture, you not only need to ensure that all your joints work as efficiently as possible, but you also need to feel properly grounded, so the position of your feet is really important. A weight-bearing joint is only mechanically balanced if the weight passes exactly through its load axis. If this is not the case, you will have to compensate by using muscle strength or by changing your posture to keep the area stable. So, when standing, your feet should be slightly apart and facing forwards or slightly outwards. Your weight should be distributed evenly throughout the soles of your feet. Try tipping forward on to your toes and then rocking back on to your heels, without lifting your foot from the floor, and then find a balance between the two. Your optimum vertical position is when your weight is evenly distributed.

Your pelvis plays an important part in achieving this balance. Try also rocking your pelvis and note how this affects the curves of your spine. When doing this, and when you play standing up, it is a good idea to keep your knees slightly bent.

Muscle and joint balance

As we get older, our abdominal muscles unfortunately get weaker and the muscles at the back of the thigh become shorter and more tense. This, of course, affects our posture, so we need to adopt a strategy that will counteract this and help us to keep a youthful posture for longer. Toning the abdominal muscles and stretching the hamstrings at the back of the leg are really helpful ways for us to achieve this. Younger musicians will also find these exercises beneficial since they help to maintain a good balance and establish good postural habits that will be of even greater benefit later in life.

The pelvic position is a key point for the balance of the spine.
Notice that as you change the pelvic tilt you also change the spine's posture.

Lie flat on your back on the floor with your hands at your sides and both knees bent up with the feet on the floor. Make sure your head, neck and shoulders are relaxed and comfortable. Straighten one leg until it is fully extended, keeping the foot flexed (the toes pulling back towards the floor). In this position, stretch the muscles at the back of the leg for 20 seconds. Repeat this two or three times with each leg. You must feel only tension, no pain. If you experience pain, reduce the stretching.

Lie flat on your back on the floor, both legs together. First, raise your right leg, with the knee bent, and push on your thigh with your right hand so that the leg resists you. Match the effort so that neither hand nor leg wins. Repeat at least 10 times with each leg and hand. Over a period of 20 days, build up to 20 times on each side. To extend this you can try crossing over and pushing the right leg with the left hand and vice versa.

Best hand position:
- Finger joints slightly bent, forming arches between them.
- Wrist in intermediate posture

Finger joints excessively bent cause tendon rubbing.

Wrist lateral deviation causes joint and nerve pinch and tendon rubbing.

Flat hand, with those joints at the base of the fingers extended, causes hand and forearm tension, tendon rubbing.

Forced or dropped wrist causes joint and nerve pinching and tendon rubbing.

Thumb in 'Z' position, although creating sensation of joint stability and more strength, causes tendon rubbing and joint stress.

Playing with a straight thumb and index finger closes the space between them. This can cause hand muscle tension and tendon rubbing.

Hyperextension of the distal part of the finger can cause joint tension and tendon rubbing.

Moreover, if your joints are placed in extreme positions, tension is placed on the ligaments and this increases the rubbing of tendons passing through the area. It is therefore very important that your joints, especially those in the upper extremities (principally the fingers, wrists and elbows), maintain an intermediate position and stay as relaxed as possible.

Basic points for good posture when playing and singing

An imaginary vertical line passing through the ear, shoulder, hip and ankle.

Proportionately this is the heaviest area of your body (your head can weigh up to 5 kg), so a good vertical position is vital. The axis of the head must be vertical. Do not push it forward or twist it as this creates tension and disequilibrium in the muscles and compresses the spinal structures.

Don't push your shoulders forward, closing the chest. Separate your shoulders from your ears, and slide your shoulder blades down your back.

Don't tense or raise your shoulders, not even to hold your instrument. Keep them symmetrical with each other. Tensing the shoulders is a common way to indicate alertness through the body, so we have to learn to be in this state but with maximum shoulder relaxation.

By keeping the ribs lifted you allow more freedom for breathing and avoid hunching.

Keep your hand and fingers, thumb included, curved as though holding a tennis ball in your palm.

Standing can over-accentuate the natural lumbar curve. Good positioning of pelvis and legs will reduce strain on the spine and muscle overload.

When in a good, relaxed standing posture, allow your arms to hang loosely by your side. Flap each of them a little and wiggle your fingers to encourage relaxation and blood flow and then allow the weight of your arm to help it to settle by your side naturally. When you are playing, your arm should not be either completely stuck to your side or too far away from your body.

To avoid exaggerating spinal curvature, find a good, central pelvic balance.

Don't compress the diaphragm and abdominal muscles excessively.

Knees should be slightly bent without tensing the legs.

Position your feet firmly on the floor, with an even distribution of your body weight: half on each leg and equally distributed between the ball and heel of each foot.

Keep your feet slightly apart and, although a separation of less than 45 degrees is acceptable, it is preferable for them to be parallel.

In sitting, an imaginary vertical line passes through the ear, shoulder and hip.

Although a slight inclination is acceptable (10 degrees), avoid looking at the floor since this is a sign that you are tipping your chin downwards. Instead fix your eyes forwards and keep them on a chosen spot as you relax into your best position.

Maintain natural curves without exaggerating them at all.

Notice if you use strong facial expression to indicate that you are alert and aim for the most relaxed state that allows you to feel comfortable. Clenched jaws and grinding teeth are signs of tension that can become habitual and so go unnoticed. They add considerably to the overall tension in the head, neck and shoulders.

If you use a chair with back support, this should cushion the lumbar area.

Remain vertical and avoid twisting and bending either forwards or backwards.

Concentrate on keeping the muscles of the forearm relaxed, especially during quick, difficult passages.

Keep the chest out of the stomach and maintain the natural lumbar curve. This aids breathing and avoids tension.

Your elbows should only be slightly in front of the body. With keyboard instruments the elbow should be a little higher than the keyboard.

Your body weight should rest only on the ischiums ❶ and not on the sacrum ❷. This allows better control of the position of your back and more freedom of movement, since you can shift your weight from one ischium to the other.

Don't compress the diaphragm and abdominal muscles excessively.

It may be helpful if the seat of the chair slopes forwards by 15–20 degrees.

The hip should be positioned slightly above the knee.

Ideally, your knees should be at an angle of 90–120 degrees. Choose a chair that assists this and change it if you need to.

Use a mirror or ask your teacher or a friend to help you to observe whether you are managing to achieve your optimum posture. Any changes must be made slowly and little by little. Always avoid making any serious changes before big performances or exams since muscles need time to readapt, and this may temporarily interfere with your performance. If, at the beginning, you find it difficult to maintain a good position without tension, you can try to begin by working while lying on the floor with your instrument or, for those bigger instruments, standing against a wall to achieve maximum possible relaxation and alignment. If you are experiencing pain through your postural control, seek the advice of a physiotherapist.

> **Warning:** Playing and singing are dynamic activities and your posture necessarily fluctuates and adapts to those demands. So, for instance, big stretches on the keyboard will affect the curves of the hand; high notes on wind and brass instruments may need raised shoulders and tense facial muscles; highlighting an electric guitar break may require you to flex your trunk and knees sharply. None of these mean that you have a poor posture if you are able to return to a good automatic position afterwards.

What is the best chair position?

If you sit for long periods, especially if you are relatively immobile, you may experience back pain. The reason is that the spinal column is subject to greater loads if you are sitting than if you maintain a good posture while standing. We therefore recommend working as much as possible by sitting and standing alternately. That is why it is important when you can take a break, to change your position, stand and walk about a bit, rather than just collapsing back into your chair.

A suitable chair is essential in order to minimise these loads as far as possible. It must perform the function of providing a stable supporting base, which enables you to adopt a good posture and gives you the freedom to play your music.

For most instruments, the chair or stool seat must be sufficiently long and wide so that your thighs are fully supported and your hips and knees are able to function at an angle greater than 90 degrees. A chair that is 1–2 inches (2–5 cm) higher than the distance between the gap behind your knee and the floor will achieve this. If necessary, books or wooden blocks can be used to raise the legs of a chair that is too small for you.

To maintain this, tension has to be applied through the back muscles to keep the lumbar curve in place. It helps to have a chair with an inclined base to keep this curve intact. As the spine is attached to the pelvis, poor posture will lead to a loss of the natural curves and the body weight will fall behind the point of support on a chair. As well as overloading the spine, this pressure compresses the abdomen leading to some restriction of abdominal breathing. This can be avoided by the aforementioned inclined chair base. As a slope greater than 20 degrees will give you the sensation of slipping forward, a slope of 15–20 degrees is recommended.

Sloping stools and chairs are available on the market (**www.ergonomic-piano-bench.com** or **www.andexinger.de**). In any case you can add a prefabricated, wedge-shaped cushion to your chair or stool (*Life-Foam Seat Cushion* **www.lifeformchairs.com**, *Ergo Sit-Rite Cushion* **www.relaxtheback.com** or *Ergo Cush* **www.alimed.com**). You can even place some blocks of wood under the back legs of the chair or inside the cover of the stool, if it has a drawer to store scores, in order to achieve this slope. The same wooden blocks can be used to level the chair if you have to play on a stage that is pitched forwards to improve the public's view.

Using a back support relieves the pressure on your back appreciably but may restrict trunk mobility. With some instruments this may be an insurmountable inconvenience. But where a support can be used it should be placed exactly against the lower part of the spine. This can provide a

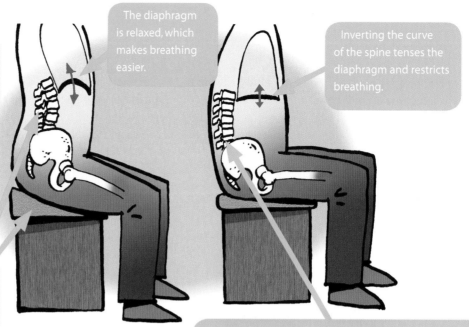

good degree of comfort without restricting mobility and interpretative freedom too much.

If you can't get hold of a sloping chair or adequate support during a performance or rehearsal, the best thing to do is to sit on the front edge of the chair. Although this reduces stability, it permits better positioning of the pelvis and, consequently, the entire back.

Going about your everyday life

Although you are a musician, you have normal daily tasks to do just like everyone else. It is perhaps easier to remember to maintain a good posture when performing or practising than when you are engaged in your daily chores. In fact, these can affect your health just as much as playing an instrument, and there are hidden dangers that are fairly easily avoided, but too often are our downfall. Just as the majority of car accidents occur near to the driver's home, so a professional musician, whose body is their work, needs to

take special care when doing normal household chores – but this doesn't mean avoiding doing them! Learning to make the movements of your everyday activities more efficient will, of course, also benefit your playing or singing.

Just as with playing and singing postures, your back is the key area during daily activities. So avoid unnecessary stretching as you get out of bed, wash and dress, and so on. Even bending over to the tap instead of using a glass of water when you clean your teeth can put you at risk. If you stand for a long time cooking or ironing, vary your position and maybe rest one foot and then the other on a raiser or, for instance, open a cupboard and put one foot on the lower shelf. Everything that makes you overstretch, especially when you are holding something heavy, can directly affect your playing if you overdo things and stretch and bend your back unnecessarily. Whatever you are doing, avoid sudden or exaggerated twisting of your back. When shopping, use a trolley rather than carrying baskets.

Lifting and carrying weights

When we speak about the loads associated with a musician's work, we usually only think about performing but we often forget those associated with lifting, transporting and assembling the instrument and its accessories. Sometimes we even have to lift and assemble the sound equipment or the stage. Therefore, if the load involved warrants it, it would be a good idea to consider using protective gloves and a lifting belt. Moreover, heavy elements should always be moved with a hand truck or cases on wheels (there are cases for cellos, double basses, tubas and drums, amongst other instruments, which have wheels and carrying handles). If you use a hand truck or a box on wheels, it is always preferable to push it with both hands instead of pulling it. If you carry it one-handed or on one shoulder, change sides often, even if the case does not weigh very much.

When lifting a weight you should always:

1. try to lift it as closely as possible to the body;

2. place your feet apart to achieve a solid support base and good balance;

3. position your feet in the direction you wish to move the object;

4. distribute the weight as symmetrically as possible;

5. bend your knees, keep your back straight and your head up;

6. lift the weight using the strength of your legs not your arms or back;

7. keep your arms close to your body;

8. lift the weight smoothly and slowly, and

9. pivot with your feet and avoid twisting your back.

How to carry your instrument

It may seem that only double bass players or harpists will need this information, but even the way you hold a piccolo case could be relevant to performance quality or could precipitate the onset of damage to your hands.

Every musician should take the following issues into account:

1. Avoid holding any weight in your hand (the instrument case, a book or a bag), however light it may seem, for too long. The sustained muscle contraction that is brought about by your grip, even though not demanding, squeezes the blood vessels that supply oxygen and nourishment to muscles and tendons. This has the potential to produce as much or even more fatigue than, for instance, playing the clarinet for half an hour. Consider buying a backpack in which to carry your instrument.

2. Whenever possible, carry the weight by hanging it on your shoulders or back. If you have to hold it with your hand, shift the weight often from one hand to the other.

3. The weight should be well distributed, using the straps of the backpack, one on each shoulder. You can buy ergonomic straps that can be added to different sizes of string- and wind-instrument cases (**www.cellofiedler.de**).

4. Hang the instrument case on your back like a rucksack. If your case does not have the right straps for this, you can buy straps that can be attached to it with simple adjustable belts using velcro (**www.bullco.net/support/case_supporting.htm**).

5. If your case has only one strap, cross it to the other shoulder and regularly change sides.

6. The straps must be wide and cushioned to avoid compression of the muscles and damage to the skin on the shoulder.

7. The straps must be adjustable to allow the instrument case to be as close as possible to your body and relatively low on your back, nearly to the buttocks, as this allows you to maintain your body's centre of gravity and reduces muscle tension.

8. If the shape of your shoulders means the straps slide off easily, you could use a case or backpack with a little belt or strip that fastens them together over your chest to avoid them separating.

9. If the weight of the instrument justifies it, use a strap that fastens the case to your waist or hips allowing transfer of an important part of the load from the shoulders and spine to a stronger area.

10. Try to carry as little weight as possible in your instrument case or backpack: buy a light case, take out those scores that you are not actually using, take only the copies of the parts you really need rather than all the books, and place the heaviest things in the part of your case or backpack that will be at the bottom and as near as possible to your body when you carry it.

11. Try to avoid carrying a backpack or instrument case that weighs more than 10% of your body weight. For example, if you weigh 60 kg (140lb) you should avoid carrying more than 6 kg (14lb) on your back. If the weight is greater than this percentage, you should consider using a system with wheels. One option is one of the cases with built-in wheels. Another possibility is a case with wheels where you can put your normal instrument case inside. You can buy a wheel set that can be easily added to your case (**www.cholley.co.uk**). Cello and double bass players can use a wheel added to the endpin.

12. It is better to push the case with wheels in front of you rather than drag it behind you. Due to its resistance, the case will remain closer to you when you push it than when you drag it, and this is better for your back. It is also easier to keep this resistance directly in front of the body rather than to one side. For these reasons, when walking down a slope you must put the case behind you.

13. Maintain a good posture when carrying a weight or your instrument case (see *Chapter 3 – Posture*).

> **Important for teachers and parents: Children and teenagers are fashion-conscious and vulnerable to peer pressure, so make sure you take your child with you when buying their case or backpack. If the style you choose is 'uncool', they may wrongly compensate by carrying it in a 'cool' way, such as over one shoulder.**

Bedtime

In our lifetime, we will all spend more time in bed than in any other one place; so make certain that the mattress is firm – neither too soft nor too hard – and will adapt to the curves of your body. Avoid sleeping in a small bed or on the sofa.

The pillow must keep the neck in alignment with the spine. The best posture is lying on your side with hips and knees bent. One or both legs may be bent. If only the top leg is bent, place a pillow under the knee to prevent twisting. If you sleep lying on your back, bend your knees. A pillow beneath the knees may help you to hold this position in a more relaxed fashion.

Musicians and computers

Working with the computer is a very common cause of physical problems. Position your chair as close to the computer table and sit at arms length from monitor. Don't lean over the table or move your head closer to the monitor. Your head should be straight and you should look only slightly downwards. The monitor and keyboard must be in front of you and, if necessary, raise the monitor by using telephone directories or something similar to place the top of the screen (not the top of the monitor) at eye level. Use a chair with a backrest and relax against it. Position the buttocks as far back on the seat as possible. Remember that, as you do when playing and singing, you should take regular breaks.

Laptops were originally designed as a temporary solution for travellers but are actually used as a daily computer by many people. As the keyboard and screen are together, if one is in an optimal position the other isn't.

Be careful to place it on a desk at the right height and, if necessary, tilt it (raise the back by placing something underneath it) so that you can see the screen without bending your neck. You could also buy a portable laptop raiser. Where possible, use it in conjunction with a separate keyboard and mouse. Avoid using your laptop in situations where your movements are constricted – which basically means never actually on your lap! If you develop a pain in your hands or back while typing, stop and seek medical advice.

❶ Keep the monitor screen perpendicular to your desk or tilted slightly upward.

❷ The height of your monitor should be such that the top of the screen (not the top of the monitor) is at eye level. A monitor raiser (phone books work well) is a good tool for adjusting the height of your monitor.

❸ Sit at arm's length from the monitor.

❹ As a minimum, a computer workstation chair should be height-adjustable.

❺ It is also recommended that chairs are equipped with adjustable arms and proper lumbar support.

❻ Adjust your chair height so that your feet rest squarely on the ground. A footrest may be useful in accomplishing this.

❼ Your thighs should be parallel to the floor, with your hips slightly higher (1 to 2 inches; 5–6 cm) than your knees. This will ensure that your bodyweight is evenly distributed along the back of your thighs.

❽ Make sure that there is little or no pressure from the seat pad on the back of your knees, as this could limit circulation.

❾ Place the centre of the chair's backrest directly at the base of your rib cage to ensure that the lumbar region of your back is adequately supported.

❿ Keep your wrists flat and straight in relation to your forearms when using the keyboard or mouse.

⓫ Position your keyboard directly in front of you. You should be able to type with your elbows resting at your sides and your head facing straight ahead.

⓬ Lay your keyboard flat on your desk. Many keyboards have tabs underneath to elevate the back. These tabs should be folded away whenever possible. You should also use a negative tilt keyboard (the top margin of the keyboard is lower than the bottom margin) to facilitate wrist relaxation.

⓭ Position the mouse within easy reach, so it can be used with the wrist straight. Support your forearm on the desk, and don't grip the mouse too tightly.

⓮ Rest your fingers lightly on the mouse's buttons. If your fingers press the buttons when you do this, you must look for another mouse with stronger button mechanisms. You should not have to press them hard.

⓯ Manoeuvre the mouse with your forearm and shoulder, not just with your hand and wrist.

⓰ Use a document holder, preferably in line with the computer screen. Place your document holder at a height and distance equal to that of your monitor, and at a location that minimises your need to turn your head to see it. Monitor-mounted document holders are best.

Quiz

1. With regard to posture, it is false that:
a) if you feel comfortable you can be sure that you have a good posture;

b) everyone has their own proper posture, but there are some general principles that must be taken into account;

c) changing posture needs time to allow muscles to adapt to the new posture and for it to become automatic.

2. With regard to posture of the spine, it is true that:
a) your spine must be straight, seen from the front and from the side;

b) the natural curves of the spine must become as pronounced as possible to avoid dangerous loads;

c) resting one foot on a raised surface will reduce the curve of the lower back and help avoid excessive spinal load.

3. To ensure good stability:
a) your weight must be on your toes to feel properly grounded;

b) changing the position of the pelvis and legs eases strain on the spine;

c) your knees must be locked to avoid involuntary movements.

4. When sitting on a chair:
a) the spinal column is subject to a smaller load than if you maintain a good posture while standing;

b) work as much as possible by sitting and standing alternately;

c) the two prior sentences are correct.

5. When you carry a weight:
a) if it is light, you can carry it one-handed or on one shoulder without changing sides often;

b) is preferable to pull a hand truck or case on wheels instead of pushing it;

c) try to lift it as closely as possible to the body.

6. When you carry your instrument, it is false that:
a) if your case only has one strap it is better to hang it on the shoulder of the same side as the case;

b) if the instrument is heavy, it is preferable to use a case with wheels;

c) the straps must be wide, cushioned and adjustable.

7. When you are working with your computer you must:
a) position your chair as near to the computer as possible;

b) not lean over the table or move your head closer to the monitor;

c) make sure the keyboard is tilted up to avoid wrist tension.

Question	Correct answer	If your answer is wrong, please read the page again and find out why you made your mistake
1	a	see page 33
2	c	see page 34
3	b	see page 34
4	b	see page 39
5	c	see page 41
6	a	see page 41
7	b	see page 42

Chapter 4

Musicians, instruments and the workplace

Adjusting the task to suit your body

Your body has a marvellous ability to adapt to the many and different situations and challenges it encounters. It is at its most adaptable when you allow changes to occur gradually over time, and also when you take great care to compensate for those changes that you have made to your body's normal routine.

Each musician's body is unique. Adaptations that may be successful for one may not be equally successful for another. You may find yourself striving to make changes beyond the capacity of your body to absorb them, with the possible results not only that you risk draining your physical resources, but also that you reduce the effectiveness of your performance. Musicians are well known for trying to force through physical changes and this is acknowledged to be a significant source of both physical problems and technical limitations.

You should learn to analyse how you can best adapt the activity of performing to your own body's needs, to make it easier, more comfortable and less harmful. This process of adaptation, based on different elements of current scientific knowledge, is known as ergonomics and may be applied to your instrument or working environment to the benefit of your performance and your health.

Changes to the instrument

In general, musicians are worried about making changes to their instruments because of the possibility that such changes may affect the way they play or their quality of sound. Some even refuse to make adaptations because they believe that using an ergonomic aid or accessory is like hanging an illuminated sign around their necks saying: 'this musician has a problem'. Others argue that all such 'contraptions' are only for beginners. But why worry about a change that could improve your abilities and prevent injuries?

We suggest that you read the ideas set out in this chapter, although they are not exhaustive or may refer to other instruments, to analyse possible weak points in your body and to begin to find ways of correcting them. Your teacher or specialist in performing arts medicine can help you with this. Begin by experimenting with small changes, and allow yourself a sensible amount of time to get used to them – this may even take several months. Evaluate the results achieved and then, if necessary, continue to experiment.

Accessories for your instrument

Removable parts are used to help to ensure that your body and your instrument make the best possible fit. Below we list the main problems so far identified and their possible solutions from an ergonomic point of view. As all of the solutions do not suit all musicians equally, we have also tried to list some of the difficulties that specialists in performing arts medicine have encountered most often. These should not be taken as problems that will be experienced by all musicians who adopt them. Some of the complaints may even result from an unwillingness to introduce changes, individual characteristics or insufficient time for adaptation to take place.

Violin, viola

Problem detected	Proposed solution	Possible drawbacks identified
● Neck bent and rotated to the left. ● Left shoulder raised and held forward. ● Tension in the shoulder muscles with a reduction in left-hand dexterity. ● Pressure on the jaw and problems with mouth articulation. ● Reduced freedom of movement in the left hand, especially in high positions.	**Chin and shoulder rest** Amongst other things, different thickness of wood, plastic, foam and inflatable pillows can be placed between the violin/viola and the shoulder or chin to make it easier to hold the instrument without lowering or twisting the head.	● Inhibits interpretation and expression as the musician's body is in a fixed position. ● Interferes with the connection between the musician and instrument. ● Affects the tonal timbre. ● Damages the instrument.
● Poor fit between the area around the chin rest and the jaw. ● Pain in the jaw or on jaw articulation.	**Chin-rest cushion** It is possible to buy a contoured gel pad that attaches via peel-and-stick adhesive to the chin rest *(GelRest*, www.gelrest.com*)*.	● Jaw pain may be the result of poor posture or tension, which the cushion will camouflage but not solve.

Cello

Problem detected	Proposed solution	Possible drawbacks identified
● The cello's neck is too far back. ● The left elbow is too bent.	**Chest rest** This attaches to the cello's purfling by means of a 'bracket' similar to that of a chin rest. The device extends from the back of the instrument and rests against the player's chest, holding the cello away from the body.	● Makes the instrument unstable. ● The right hand is further from the body making the right shoulder work harder.
● The cello's tuning pegs interfere with the correct position and mobility of the head. ● To avoid this, the bow has to be held at an excessive distance.	**Removable peg** Removable tuning key for the G and C strings is available that allows one to tune the cello and then remove the bulky part of the peg that protrudes from the peg box (Posture Peg http://www.cellos2go.com).	● Fear of losing the tuning peg. ● Impossible to tune the instrument during the concert if the pegs have been left in the dressing room.

Bowed string instrument

Problem detected	Proposed solution	Possible drawbacks identified
● Pain or numbness in the fingers of the right hand where they press on the bow tightly.	**Bow protector** This is an open rubber tube, which is placed on the bow to smooth hard edges and reduce slipping.	● Reduces feeling and bow control.

Problem detected	Proposed solution	Possible drawbacks identified

Guitar

<table>
<tr>
<td>

- The foot-rest causes excessive left knee and hip flexion as well as high tension in the lumbar area, and prevents balanced and stable positioning of the feet on the ground.

- All of this makes correct posture difficult to achieve and may cause injuries.

</td>
<td>

Guitar support

There are parts made in different materials, some of which are height and angle adjustable, that lift the guitar without the need to raise the leg (*A-Frame and Ergoplay* www.xguitars.com; *Arm'n'track* www.hernestudios.co.uk; *Dynarette Support Cushion* www.vamu.se; *Efel* www.efelmusic.com; *Gitano Guitar Support*; *Iarkit* www.guitarras-madrigal.com; *NeckUp* www.neckup.com).

</td>
<td>

- The finish on certain guitars may react with the suction cups used by some guitar supports and leave a mark on the guitar (there are ways of protecting the guitar: www.kling-on.com).

- Not all these supports are suitable for solid-body electric guitars.

- Some of them are cumbersome to carry around.

- The guitar is in a very vertical position and has little contact with the body.

- The guitar position changes.

- The guitar is not as stable.

- The sound of the guitar changes as there is something stuck to the soundbox instead of the instrument being in contact with the thigh.

</td>
</tr>
</table>

Plucked string instruments

<table>
<tr>
<td>

- The action of changing strings or turning tuning pegs can cause excessive and unequal pressure on the small finger joints, producing discomfort in the fingers, hands, wrist or forearm, especially if there is already an injury in these areas.

</td>
<td>

Stringwinders

These are pieces that are connected to the tuning peg and make the movement quicker and easier and enable it to be performed without having to twist the joints. They usually have a bulkier handle for a more natural grip (*Ernie Ball String Winder, Ergonomic Tuning Key, Jim Dunlop Ergonomic String Winder, Guitar & Bass Ergo Stringwinder, Shubb W-1 Stringwinder, Spin Doctor String Winder*).

</td>
<td>

- Some models easily jump off the peg.

</td>
</tr>
</table>

47

Flute

- Because of the design and position of some of the flute's mechanisms, it tends to rotate towards the musician's palm in open positions such as C#. To compensate for this instability, there is a tendency to apply greater pressure with the fingers on the flute and the flute on the lips.

- Excessive pressure may cause problems in the fingers, lips, teeth and the jaw joint.

- The flute becomes unstable when moving between octaves.

Flute rest

- A platform fitted to the shape of the thumb is fixed to the flute using removable systems, which does not damage the flute. The platform prevents the flute rolling and helps the hand to maintain the correct position. Although they are mainly designed for the right hand, there are also left-hand models (*Stedirest*).

- They also increase the contact area between the flute and finger reducing pressure and increasing comfort (*Prima right-hand thumbrest* **www.tonkooiman.com**; *Thumbalina Thumb Rest* **http://home.nethere.net/roger45/Thumbalina_Flute_Thumb_Rest_Support.htm**).

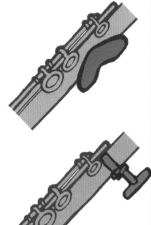

- To achieve a good grip with the left hand, the base of the index finger must be in contact with the flute.

- This usually involves a forced position of the index finger, thumb and wrist.

- Contact of the hand and finger with the flute can cause injuries, especially in an area where finger nerves are rooted.

Spacers

Spacers are plastic parts that are affixed to the body of the flute in the area where a finger makes contact with the instrument. Some are slim and work simply by cushioning and preventing slipping (*Non-Slip Flute Cushions* **www.runyonproducts.com**). Thicker ones help the fingers to stay in a more arched position, meaning the wrist is less rotated and the flute more secure, and they prevent contact between the finger and the hand with the pronounced curve of the flute (*Flute Hand Rest* **www.runyonproducts.com**; *Stedirest Bo-pep Finger Saddle and Finger Rest*).

- They can slide around and interfere with the keys.

- They leave small scratches on the flute when removed.

Problem detected	Proposed solution	Possible drawbacks identified

Recorder

- Tends to be unstable when playing notes requiring the use of only one finger on the left hand.

- Possibility of the recorder slipping when it is played in a very vertical position, especially with larger instruments. This usually involves adopting uncomfortable positions or excessive tension to maintain the instrument's position.

Thumb rest

It is possible to use a removable plastic part, which attaches to the body of the recorder in the desired area, making it easier to hold – this allows the hand to assume a more comfortable and relaxed posture. The resulting improved grip makes it possible to play more freely and quickly. The rest also has the advantage during classes of preventing the recorder from rolling on the table and falling on the floor. It acts as a guide to help the right hand return to its exact position. *(www.courtlymusicunlimited. com/Accessories.html; www.rhythmband. com/aulosrec3.html)*.

- Some models may damage wooden recorders.

- It can encourage a tendency to play the instrument in an excessively vertical position that may affect sound, technique and posture.

- It can make some virtuoso techniques difficult.

Woodwind instruments

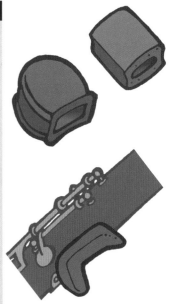

- The metal thumb rest has a poor fit with the shape of the finger causing discomfort in the pressure zones.

- Calluses develop in the pressure zones.

Thumb rest cushion

A small piece of rubber attached to the thumb rest can distribute pressure more evenly and prevent slipping.

- It may make it difficult to get a good grip on the instrument.

- Some are too hard or small and do not distribute the pressure well.

- Some models tend to fall off because of the movement of the strap and are lost.

- In order to achieve a solid and stable support, there is a tendency to shorten the distance between the index finger and thumb of the right hand too much.

- This overloads the finger joints and muscles and/or irritates tendons.

Thumb rest

A wider and thicker thumb rest can increase the contact area with the thumb and open the space between the thumb and index finger *(Ridenour Clarinet Thumb Saddle www.ridenourclarinetproducts.com)*.

- Changes the sound of the instrument.

- Some of these thumb rests require new holes to be made in the clarinet to fit them.

- Not all of them make it possible to hang the sling.

Problem detected	Proposed solution	Possible drawbacks identified

- Playing some keys involves twisting the palm of the hand or the wrist.

Key risers

Small rubber or metal parts attached to the keys make them easier to access with the palm or side of the hand. As they are removable, they avoid permanent changes to the instrument *(Oleg Side and Palm Key Risers* **www.olegproducts.com**; *Runyon Side and Palm Key Risers* **www.runyonproducts.com***).*

- Rubber risers tend to lose their firmness after some months of use.
- They rub the finish off the keys and leave a residue on them.
- They dampen the tone and resonance.

Horn

- It is difficult for small hands to perform a good handstop on the bell of the horn.
- Placing the hand too far into the bell means that it has to work in a forced position causing muscle tension.

Silicone handstop

This is a piece of silicone fitted between the thumb and index finger that provides thickness and prevents slipping (**www.pyp.f2s.com**).

- Must be hand-made and shaped to the owner's hand.

Brass instruments

- If mouthpieces are left for a long time on an instrument, they stick to it and become difficult to remove.
- Their removal can involve significant effort or the risk of receiving a blow or adopting a forced posture, especially for instrument repairers or conductors.

Mouthpiece puller

An extraction tool, adaptable to different instruments and sizes of instruments, can remove the mouthpiece (*Bobcat Mouthpiece Puller,* **www.bill-lewington.com/bobcat.htm**; *DEG Magnum Mouthpiece Puller* **www.degaccessories.com**; *Valentino Jr Mouthpiece Puller*).

Singers

- Holding the musical score during a rehearsal or concert involves some tension and load for the hands and arms.
- There is a risk of dropping the score when turning the page. This causes greater tension and makes it difficult to concentrate on performing.

Choral folder with handle

A handle on the back of the choral folder can alleviate this problem (*Manhasset Choral Folder* **www.manhasset-specialty.com**).

Transfer and improved distribution of weight

The heavy weight of certain instruments, such as the saxophone or the bassoon, means that few people would argue about the need to use straps to support them and thus remove part of the load from the fingers and hands. However, although there is currently a wide range of options in the market, some straps cause tension in the neck and shoulders or compress sensitive areas.

As a general design principle, the strap must:

● be wide

● be well padded

● be adjustable

● be able to adapt to individual anatomical differences (e.g. women's chests)

● distribute the load as symmetrically as possible

● preferably rest on the strongest areas of the body (it is better to load the neck area then the fingers, better still the shoulders and even better the waist).

Let's look at other examples of how the load-bearing zone can be changed.

Problem to be corrected	Proposed solution	Possible drawbacks identified
Transfer weight to the hand		
● The end of the thumb on the right hand supports the majority of the weight of woodwind instruments. ● This may cause tension and pain in the thumb, hand, wrist and forearm.	**Thumb rest** It is possible to obtain thumb rests with a support that transfer part of the weight of the instrument to the base of the thumb or the first commissure. As they are thicker and wider than conventional thumb rests, they increase the contact area and open up the space between the first finger and the rest of the hand (*Thumb rests for clarinet, sax and oboe*, www.tonkooiman.com).	● Instrument imbalance. ● Some of these thumb rests require new holes in order to fit them. ● Some do not have a ring on which to hang the sling. 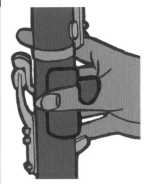
● Holding the horn may cause tension and unnecessary load on the left hand, especially the little finger. ● This may limit the mobility of the fingers over the valves.	**Left-hand support** A small bar, which is attached to the horn, allows the weight of the instrument to be supported on the soft part of the first commissure. The same thing can be achieved with a handle attached to the instrument using velcro straps (*http://hornmouthpiece.com*; www.clebschstrap.com).	

Problem to be corrected	Proposed solution	Possible drawbacks identified

Transfer weight to the body

● However well padded straps are, they may overload the muscles on the lateral part of the neck and shoulder, especially if the weight rests only on one side. ● An asymmetrical load contributes to back problems. ● Pressure on some parts of the shoulder can cause pain and irritate the nerves that pass through the area.	**Spread the load over both shoulders** 1. A second Y-shaped belt can stabilise the instrument and distribute the weight of the guitar or bass over both shoulders (*Y strap*, http://pages.infinit.net/ystrap; *Dare strap*, www.idare2.com). 2. A double strap with a sliding belt allows the instrument to move without interfering with the symmetrical distribution of weight over both shoulders. These can also be used for percussion instruments, banjo, saxophone, etc. (*Dual Slider Percussion Straps*, www.remo.com; *Slider-straps* www.slider-straps.com).	● Some straps position the instrument too far to the right or left, making it uncomfortable for the wrist, elbow or shoulder. There are accessories that help to centre the instrument (*Coracor* www.arts-medicine.com). ● With some accessories the instrument is attached too tightly to the body, which creates difficulties for musicians who have to change position or fit the instrument between colleagues on small stages.
● Tension tends to build up in the shoulders and neck muscles, both when playing and in everyday life. If you transfer the weight of the instrument on to them, your situation may get worse and problems may appear that make it difficult to perform.	**Transfer the weight to the chest and waist** ● Some support systems transfer the weight partially or totally to the chest or waist. Some use straps that pass round both the neck and waist. Others are based on devices that rest on the chest or attach to the waist itself. ● They are also useful for playing in a sitting or standing position and there are models for guitars, basses, and woodwind and brass instruments (*BassBrace*, www.bassbrace.com; *Ergobone*, www.ergobone.com; *SAMI*, www.quodlibet.com; *Smart strap* www.smartstrap.com; *Schulman System*, www.shulmansystem.com).	● Some models cause an imbalance in the instrument. ● A feeling that the instrument is too rigid or too close to the body. ● Some devices have a poor fit with women's body shapes.

Problem to be corrected	Proposed solution	Possible drawbacks identified
	Transfer the weight to the thigh With instruments such as the horn or saxophone, where the instrument is held to one side, a support may be used to transfer the weight to the thigh (*PipStick* **www.pyp.f2s.com**).	

Transfer weight to a chair

• You should always try to use the strongest parts of the body when trying to transfer the weight of a woodwind or brass instrument. If possible, this should be away from the body. • When the weight is transferred to the shoulders or the waist, the instrument may sit too close to the body or give the musician the feeling of restricted movement.	**Chair stand** Height adjustable bars fixed to the thumb rest or other areas of the woodwind or brass instrument can transfer the weight of the instrument to a chair (*FHRED*, **www.quodlibet.com**; *Stewart Tuba Stand*; *Tuba Rest*, **www.wengercorp.com**).	• Can constrict expressive movement of the instrument.

Transfer weight to the floor

• The shape of the instrument or the way it is played does not enable the weight to be transferred effectively to the body and chair. • In such cases or when the load on the body causes problems, transferring the weight to the floor may be a good option.	**Stand** • Adjustable supports that use a tripod or other stabilisation system on the floor to take the instrument's weight are available. • There are stands for many instruments such as the guitar, bass, bass clarinet, tuba and other woodwind and brass instruments (*BHEN y CASI*, **www.quodlibet.com**; *DEG Tuba Stands*, **www.degaccessories.com**; *Gracie PS-A Performer Guitar Stand* **www.edromanguitars.com**; *Konig and Meyer Tuba Rest*; *Mbrace Guitar Support System*; *Tuba Tamer*, **www.wengercorp.com**; *Vonk*, **www.fagot.nl**).	• The instrument is in too fixed a position, which may cause a stiff, tense posture to be adopted. • The base or tripod of some models may make it difficult to find a correct, comfortable position for the feet and body. • Some models break quite easily as they lack stiffness and strength. • Some devices are heavy and not very portable.

Problem to be corrected	Proposed solution	Possible drawbacks identified

Endpin

Some instruments (such as the English horn, bassoon or bass recorder, for example) may have an endpin fitted similar to that on a cello to transfer the weight to the floor (*Bassoon Support*, **www.forrestsmusic. com**; *Shaw bass recorder universal floor rest*, **www.courtlymusicunlimited. com/Accessories/Floor-rest.html**).

Modifying the instrument

For centuries, instrument makers have sought ways to adapt instruments for disabled musicians (people with amputated fingers, paralysed hands, traumatic or genetic deformities, etc.). The results are often surprising (**www.flutelab.com**). If we really can adapt instruments to address these enormous limitations, why not try to do the same with your minor imbalances so as to stop them eventually turning into major ones?

Examples of small changes

Often the conductor of the orchestra or group dictates what size an instrument should be, but the sole deciding factor ought to be the size of the musician who has to play it. This is possible with many stringed instruments, for example, where characteristics such as length, distance between strings and the size of the body can be changed.

As the musical world demands increasing diversity and flexibility in professional musicians (in early music, theatre pit orchestras and so on), it becomes more important that performers should be aware of the potential for strain that changing between one instrument and another during a performance can bring.

For woodwind instruments

● Make the keys longer to prevent fingers having to stretch too much to reach them (for example modify the A, G and G# keys on the flute to improve access and posture for musicians with small hands). These modifications can even be made using plastic clips or removable metal parts (*Brannen Brothers Flute Makers*, **www.brannenflutes.com**).

● Change the space between the discs to avoid tension between the fingers.

For brass instruments

● Shape the trombone tube so that it fits the profile of the shoulder. This reduces the pressure zones and makes it easier for young or smaller musicians to hold the instrument and position the arms and mouthpiece correctly (*Jupiter 438 Ergonomic*, **www.jupitermusic.com**).

● Attach a part to the trombone slide so that it can be played closer to the body (*DEG Slide Extension*, **www.degaccessories. com**).

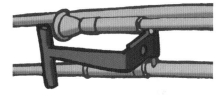

● Tilt the mouthpiece of the horn down by 8 degrees. This avoids the need to bend the neck in order to position the mouth correctly or to raise both the instrument and the arms (**www.pyp.f2s.com**).

● Change the valve height to allow better adjustment for the differences between fingers. It also makes sense to change the position of the valves into a more curved arrangement, as the length of each finger is different.

For stringed instruments

- Shorten the body. Although the conformed-to-heel cutaway for easy access to the upper fingerboard is most common, rounding off the upper edge of the guitar or bass may be considered to avoid excessive pressure on the right forearm, the structure of which is extremely sensitive to pressure. This rounding-off effect may also be achieved by attaching protective parts to the guitar (*Armrest and Ribrest*, **www.williamlaskin.com**; *Plenosom Armrest*, **www.bellinati.com**).

- Reduce the width of the upper part of the soundbox to provide better access for the right arm over the guitar. As it appears that one of the most important factors for sound quality is the amount of air within the soundbox, make the bottom side wider than normal to compensate for the loss (*Cumpiano Wedge guitars*, **www.cumpiano.com/Home/Guitars/Special/Wedge/wedge.htm**).

Other examples

- Round off the edges of the holes of the harmonica to improve movement and avoid chafing (*Renaissance Chromatic Harmonica*, **www.angelfire.com/music/HarpOn/reviewscust.html**).

- Angle the endpin of a cello or double bass so that the instrument is in a more horizontal position. This allows the weight of the bowing hand to be used more and in a more relaxed way, and reduces the rotation of the left hand.

- Change the centre of gravity of drumsticks so that rotation is better balanced (*Rotationally Balanced Drumsticks*, **www.rbstix.com**).

Examples of substantial changes

Some instrument makers are beginning to use new materials such as carbon fibre to make flutes, the fingerboards of string instruments or bows, as it is a material that, in addition to offering good acoustic and strength properties, is much lighter. Similarly, the practicality of making fingerboards out of polymers is being examined in an attempt to reduce the amount of vibration that is transmitted to the hand with each stroke.

For wind and brass instruments

- Change the fingering of the flute or saxophone so that successive chromatic notes are produced by closing the following key with the next finger of the same hand in a linear sequence. This makes both learning and performing easier (**http://draco.its.csufresno.edu/~js210**).

- Angle the head joint of the flute. The way that the flute is played involves distancing the right elbow or bending and rotating the head. As neither of these is healthy, several instrument makers are making angled, or even vertical, flutes. As some of these models increase the instability of the flute, they are usually played in conjunction with the thumb rests we saw earlier (*Drelinger's UpRite*, **http://drelinger.com/brochure/uprite_brochure1.htm**; *Emerson SS 30 Angled Flute Head Joint, Swan-neck and Vertical flute*, **www.flutelab.com**; *Yamaha Curved Head Joint*).

For string instruments

- Position the guitar strings off-centre in a lower position in relation to the body of the instrument to allow an improved wrist and right-hand position. The same can be done with the violin and viola, enabling them to be played more comfortably in high left-hand positions with better access for the bow (**www.rivinus-instruments.com**).

- Twist the neck of the guitar or bass to avoid excessive flexion in the wrist in a lower position, especially when using a capo. Necks are even sold separately for attachment to guitars (*Lace Helix Twisted Neck*, **www.agi-lace.com**).

Warning: Even if an instrument has been modified to improve its overall ergonomics, this does not necessarily mean that it will suit you. The requirements of each particular case should be evaluated and you should analyse whether a particular ergonomic design is the right one for you.

On the other hand, any change, whether to improve ergonomics or posture, requires some getting used to. You should not judge the results of modifying an instrument immediately but allow for a transition period. Where major changes are involved you should even consider a period of progressive adaptation (initially playing for a short time, slowly and with an easy repertoire, progressing gradually over a period of days).

It is not advisable to introduce changes when you are experiencing pain. The injury will stop you from reaching the correct judgement about the change's suitability and the process of adaptation may cause the injury to get worse. So, first get rid of the pain and then, by analysing the causes of the problem, carry out the appropriate modifications to your instrument or accessories.

Modifying accessories

To achieve peak performance (to be able to play with optimal efficiency and without symptoms of fatigue) and minimise the risk of injuring your body, you should also consider how to use, adjust and position musical accessories.

Chair

Guidelines about chairs are provided on page 39 and page 43 (computer section).

Music stand

Although the eye can tolerate viewing scores at an angle of up to 30 degrees, it works most comfortably when scores are placed around 15 degrees below the horizontal. For this reason, in order to avoid tired eyes or having to excessively bend the head, you should place the score at 23–27 inches (60–70 cm) from your body (or at arm's length from you) and between 6 inches (15 cm) – for the score's first line – and 27 inches (70 cm) – for the score's last line – below your eyes, keeping your neck straight when taking these measurements.

Score

To prevent tired eyes, avoid mistakes and ensure correct reading speed, the quality of the score is very important. If the quality of the paper and print is not good, a score may lose up to 50% of its readability in five years. It is therefore desirable to replace the score with a new one before this deterioration affects your health and performance. As well as possibly being illegal, using photocopies is not really very helpful either if they are not of a high quality.

Changing the environment

Lighting

When it comes to thinking about how to light your work area, the basic aim is to provide a level of illumination that is sufficient but that does not cause reflections, shining or dazzling. If the lighting design is correct, peak performance efficiency will be achieved while delaying the onset of tiredness.

As a general principle, you should consider the following as best practice:

1. The best option is natural lighting, but not if it is too bright, and the window must not be in front of you. If necessary you could completely or partially close the curtains or put a board in front of the window.

2. If natural lighting is not possible, use general electric lighting (for example, ceiling-based, white, warm fluorescent lighting) rather than lights focused directly on the work area.

3. Lighting for the score should be around 500 lux (although this depends on the distance and the characteristics of the room – this can be achieved by using a 100-watt lamp – or two of 50 watts – fitted to the ceiling).

4. If you use fluorescent lights, you should bear in mind that they have a long but not infinite life and that, before they go completely, there may be many months where the light is flickering almost imperceptibly but

Lighting: It is better to use diffused general lighting. Fluorescent lights, about a total of 100 watts in a small room, are enough.

Dazzling: If lights do not have a diffuser, they should not be placed more than 45° from the vertical with respect to our line of sight. The fluorescent tube should preferably be positioned to one side of the musician, parallel to the body.

Local lighting: This is not the most suitable. If a music stand light is used, you should remember that the ratio with general lighting should be 10:1 at most (the stand being lit 10 times more brightly than the room).

Reflection: Avoid bright areas in front of the eyes (windows, spotlights) or walls or features which may cause excessive light reflection.

Curtains: It is a good idea to hang thick curtains on windows or adjustable blinds (preferably vertical) to control the entry of light. Curtains also help to reduce noise.

Temperature and humidity: Keep the room between 20 and 24°C in summer and between 21 and 23°C in winter. Humidity should be between 40% and 60%. Air speed should not exceed 0.25 m/s in summer or 0.15 m/s in winter.

Music stand: The eye works most comfortably when scores are placed around 15° below the horizontal. Place the score at 60–70 cm from your body.

Panels: A panel or screen helps avoid dazzling. It will also help to reduce sound pressure, especially if covered in a material such as cork.

45°

15–30°

---

in a way that is very tiring. Check them from time to time and replace them when necessary.

5. Fluorescent lights should not be bare – you should fit diffuser panels to prevent dazzling.

6. Light should preferably come from the side.

7. You should not place any unscreened light source more than 40 degrees below the vertical.

Using local lighting (for example, over the music stand) presents two problems you should consider. Firstly, it may cause reflections on the score; secondly, but more particularly, it causes too great a difference in light compared to the surroundings. This will assist your concentration but, if the difference is too great, will mean that you may experience visual fatigue more easily (feeling of tired eyes, oversensitivity to light, itching, irritation and soreness of the eyes, giddiness, watery eyes, blurred or double vision, headaches, etc.). One situation you should particularly think about in this respect is the one where you are playing in the orchestra pit with a low level of general lighting and having to look alternately at the score and the conductor. You should try to ensure that the ratio between the lighting of conductor and your score does not exceed 1:3 (so the lighting on your score is not more than three times brighter than that on the conductor).

Ambient temperature

A comfortable temperature is defined as a situation where the heat produced by your own body is balanced with the heat it loses. Each instrument involves a different level of physical activity, the heat generated by the body reduces with age and everybody has an individual preference with regards to temperature, so it is difficult to find a temperature to suit all tastes.

In general, a temperature of between 21 and 23 degrees Celsius in winter and between 20 and 24 degrees Celsius in summer should be considered as suitable for most musicians.

The clothes you wear are also important since, according to the amount of body surface covered and the type of cloth, they determine the ease with which heat is exchanged between your body and the environment. Thus, for example, a cap may prevent significant loss of body warmth and while two suits appear the same, one may be made from wool (offering very good insulating properties) and the other from polyester (which has a greater heat exchange capacity).

The level of atmospheric humidity is also important when it comes to ensuring a high degree of comfort. An atmosphere that is too dry, for example because of air conditioning, will dry the mucous lining of the respiratory tract (see page 71), causing dryness in the nose and throat (usually the first symptom of the problem), which may become a painful inflammation. If we continue to be exposed to the dry atmosphere, it will become difficult to speak and to swallow.

Gradually the mucous in the respiratory tract will become thicker, making it more difficult to stop germs and allowing infections to develop.

This will be much more significant for singers, and brass and woodwind players, who breathe a greater amount of air in and out.

As a general rule, it is advisable for the humidity in heated rooms to be between 40% and 60%. In summer, a more suitable level of humidity would be between 40% and 45%.

Sound

The ear is joined to other neural areas by its connections with the brain in order for us to hear (see page 22). If the stimulation is sufficiently intense, whether from rock or classical music, these neural areas provoke reactions such as an increase in muscle tone, changes in the digestive tract or an increase in heart rate, blood pressure and reaction times. If this occurs continually it may also cause problems such as headaches, nausea, irritability, stress, insomnia and impaired performance. But the most well-known harmful effect of noise is the loss of hearing.

What determines the degree of harm it causes?

Three factors determine how harmful a noise may be: (1) sound pressure (which is measured in decibels (dBA), often known as volume), (2) sound frequency (we know that at the same pressure a high-pitched sound is more harmful than a low-pitched sound) and (3) exposure time (while it is accepted that we can tolerate up to 80 dBA for eight hours a day without significant repercussions, we can only tolerate 135 dBA if the exposure time is short).

Although safety levels are usually defined according to the amount of decibels to which your ear is subjected during one day or one week, the impact that peaks of sound pressure may have should not be underestimated. For example, peaks of almost 140 dBA in symphony orchestras and 150 dBA in rock groups are not unusual.

Sound pressure reduces significantly the further you

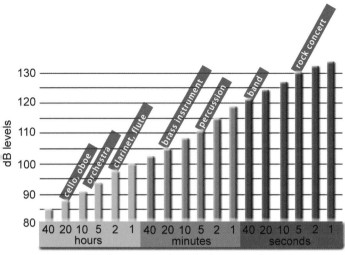

dB levels

130
120
110
100
90
80

| 40 20 10 5 2 1 | 40 20 10 5 2 1 | 40 20 10 5 2 1 |
| hours | minutes | seconds |

cello, oboe
orchestra
clarinet, flute
brass instrument
percussion
band
rock concert

Total exposure time during a week

are from the source of noise. For this reason, hearing is usually worse in the left ear of violin and viola players and percussionists, while the right ear is worst affected in flautists.

What are its possible effects on hearing?

Although the main injury to the ear is loss of hearing through damage to the auditory cells, exposure to excessive noise can also lead to whistling or buzzing (tinnitus), reduced tolerance of noise, distortion or a lack of clarity and distortion in the timbre of sounds.

All of these problems usually manifest themselves in subtle ways with no alarm signals but can be the beginning of permanent problems. In addition, although loss of hearing can be improved using certain devices, it is difficult to return the quality of hearing to normal – there are no medicines or therapies to correct damaged hearing. This could affect your professional performance and also your enjoyment of music.

However, the idea that these problems are inevitable for a musician is wrong. To look after your hearing, assess your risks and adopt any measures necessary to avoid or minimise problems.

Who should protect their hearing?

We know that up to half of professional classical musicians have detectable hearing problems. In addition, older school pupils who play in bands are more than twice as likely to have problems compared with those who do not play in bands.

The best way to find out whether you are at risk is to measure the sound pressure to which you are exposed. There are sound meters available for this purpose at very reasonable prices. If you do not have access to this measurement, specialists advise that you ask yourself the following questions:

● When I play, do I have to raise my tone of voice so that others can hear me?

● Do my ears temporarily ring after performances?

● Does everything around me sound muffled after a show or rehearsal?

● Do my ears ever feel plugged up after playing?

● Do my ears sometimes feel full or stopped up at other times?

● Does my music sound distorted?

● Do I have family members with hearing loss?

If you answered 'yes' to any one of these questions, then you could be at risk of damaging your hearing.

How can you reduce the impact of noise?

Think about one or, better still, several of these options:

1. Play more softly. Although this is not always feasible, it is the first option to consider.

2. Reduce your performance time (in addition to being impractical, this is also usually ineffective since reducing exposure by 3 dBA requires reducing the time by half).

3. Incorporate 'quiet breaks' (for example, 15 minutes every 2 or 3 hours of playing or one or two days of rest for your ears after being exposed to high noise levels). This will allow any damage to the inner ear to repair itself or avoid the recently damaged zones, which are most sensitive to sound attack, being damaged irreparably.

4. Stay away from sound sources that are potentially damaging (for example, if the dimensions of the rehearsal hall allow, increase your distance from other musicians or loudspeakers).

5. Position the musicians who make the most noise strategically, for example, by avoiding placing musicians in front of the brass section or, in any case, raising the brass musicians on a daïs so that the damaging energy they produce passes over the heads of those in front.

6. Choose an appropriate repertoire for the characteristics of the room where you are going to play. If the stage is very small (meaning that the musicians will have to be very close together) or the seating will reflect the sound to a high degree, it would be best to avoid loud pieces.

7. Place sound barriers. There are methacrylate screens that can be positioned around the drums or in front of brass musicians to protect the string section. You should remember that these panels do not absorb sound. Depending on how they are placed they may reflect and increase the auditory impact on the player of that instrument (**www.wengercorp.com, www.drumcentral.com, www.drumshields.com**).

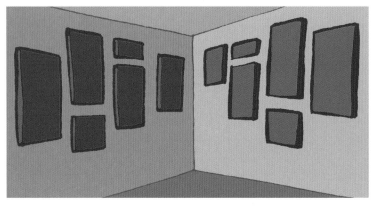

8. Improve the acoustics of the rehearsal or performance hall. Although there are absorbent plates and panels and sound diffusers, which are easy to fix to the walls or ceiling (**www.wengercorp.com, www.amadeus-acousticsolutions.co.uk**), or folding acoustic screens, there are also other measures that can easily be implemented. For example, absorbent materials such as cork boards, curtains or rugs can be used.

9. Use musicians' earplugs. Conventional earplugs reduce high frequencies more than low and medium frequencies. This means that the voice and music sound indistinct and unnatural. For this reason, there are earplugs especially designed for musicians, which offer different degrees of sound reduction without distorting it (**www.etymotic.com, www.sensaphonics.com, www.earplugco.com, www.hear-more.com, www.westone.com**). There is a wide range of hearing protection available and each individual must find the model that best suits their needs. The best comfort is provided by those made to measure. If the latter are fitted into the deepest part of the auditory canal (the bony section), the so-called occlusion effect – which causes a hollow or booming sound when one is speaking, singing or playing a brass or wind instrument – can be avoided. The table shows you how the healthy exposure time varies (expressed in hours per day) according to noise level and the degree of protection used.

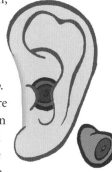

Noise Level (dB)	Without Protection	10 dB Protection	15 dB Protection	20 dB Protection
95	¾	8	more than 8	more than 8
100	¼	2½	8	more than 8
105	0	¾	2½	8
110	0	¼	¾	2½

Musicians often ask

What level of protection does an in-ear monitor offer? *We should bear in mind that in-ear monitors (high-fidelity miniature speakers inserted into custom ear moulds that provide individual control for each musician over the instrumental and vocal mix) are not designed to be hearing-protection devices. So we should remember that, although some in-ear monitors offer a reduction of up to 20 dBA of noise, these monitors are able to produce sound levels equal to or even greater than floor monitors. In order for in-ear monitors to be effective they must provide acoustic isolation from external sound while providing the full dynamic range of the music without exposure to ear-shattering levels. It would therefore be best to consult an ear specialist in order to control the sound pressure produced by the in-ear monitor correctly.*

Quiz

1. Ergonomic musical instruments are:
   a) only for handicapped or injured musicians;
   b) only for beginners;
   c) for those who want to improve their abilities and prevent injuries.

2. Straps for instruments must:
   a) be thin to adapt easily to individual differences;
   b) distribute the load as symmetrically as possible;
   c) rest on the more mobile areas of the body to allow better weight distribution.

3. A lighting design should consider:
   a) the use of lights focused directly on the work area;
   b) that lights should preferably come from the side;
   c) the use of bare fluorescent lights to avoid dazzling.

4. If sufficiently intense, sound could produce:
   a) increase in muscle tone, blood pressure and headaches;
   b) damage to the auditory cells, but only if you are exposed for a very long time;
   c) reduced tolerance to noise, but only in hard-rock musicians.

Warning: Do not assume that the absence of whistling (tinnitus) means that your ears are healthy. The majority of musicians who suffer from hearing loss have never previously experienced whistling. Therefore, do not forget to have your ears examined at least once a year. The specialist has tools to detect not only incipient problems but also your ears' ability to tolerate noise.

5. The factors that determine how harmful a noise may be are:
   a) type of music and ear size;
   b) sound pressure and exposure time;
   c) sound pressure, sound frequency and exposure time, all together.

6. You could reduce the hearing damage risk by:
   a) incorporating 'quiet breaks';
   b) staying close to sound sources;
   c) removing curtains from the rehearsal room.

Question	Correct answer	If your answer is wrong, please read the page again and find out why you made your mistake
1	c	see page 45
2	b	see page 51
3	b	see page 57
4	a	see page 58
5	c	see page 58
6	a	see page 59

Chapter 5
The musician's body explained

This chapter will deal with some of the essential elements of a musician's body so as to give us some understanding of the mechanics of performance (*see Chapter 1 – Basic functions*). The chapter is intended to be very factual, but, to make it as easy as possible to understand, we will only provide those details that musicians really need to know. Please read it carefully and try to understand the basics so that you may make the best use of your body.

Your skeleton – basic information

Bones ❶

Bones provide the support we need, give us shape and allow our muscles to perform. They are made of tissue wrapped in a mineralised substance (principally calcium). This mixture gives our bones almost the strength of iron, but they are three times lighter and ten times more flexible. They also act as a protective shell for organs such as the brain or the heart and lungs. Bones are living structures and their cells are constantly being created and destroyed. So, if a particular part of your body is placed under a greater load, bone cells will automatically reinforce its structure, but if use decreases (for example, if you are immobilised by a plaster cast) or if your diet contains a low level of calcium, the mineral component may be absorbed and your bones will become weaker as a result.

Joints ❷

Joints are where two or more bones meet. There are three kinds of joint:

Synovial (for example, elbow): its function is to allow movement between two bones. To make this happen as smoothly as possible, the contact surfaces are covered with a smooth tissue that is resistant to wear (articular cartilage). This cartilage is lubricated by a tiny quantity of viscous liquid (synovial fluid), produced by the joint covering (the synovial capsule), which reduces friction and wear and tear. The synovial fluid nourishes the cartilage and enters and is squeezed out from inside the cartilage with each movement.

Musicians often ask

Can I avoid bone decalcification? *Although bones have a tendency to lose calcium after the age of forty, calcium formation must be stimulated, from puberty onwards, through a balanced diet, moderate physical activity (walking, dancing, skating, running, etc. a minimum or two or three times a week) and avoiding the consumption of toxins (alcohol, tobacco and coffee, which leach calcium). This applies to both sexes but it is especially important in women.*

Outside the joint covering there are stronger tissues known as ligaments, which strengthen it and restrict certain movements partially or completely. If the ligaments are more flexible than normal, you may find you can move your joints more than other people can. This is known as hypermobility or double-jointedness – sometimes referred to as hyperlaxity or hyperflexibility. Although this could be a technical advantage, hypermobile musicians need more muscular effort to control and hold their joints in the correct position, and this could become a health problem if not accurately compensated by muscle work (see page 64).

Cartilaginous: these have a fibrous structure that, in addition to allowing flexible movement (for example, between the ribs and the sternum), cushions impacts and loads (for example, a vertebral disc).

Fibrous (for example, between the bones of the pelvis or skull): these have little movement and simply acts as a point of connection.

Muscle ❸

Muscle is also tissue, which we can contract. Muscles connected to bones can be contracted voluntarily and produce movement. As we have seen in Chapter 1, muscles are formed by thousands of elongated cells which are called muscle fibres. These may be thick (responsible for slow and powerful movements such as those of the right leg of a drummer pressing the bass drum pedal) or thin (they operate during fast, short movements requiring little power as those of the right-hand fingers plucking the guitar strings). According to its function, each muscle naturally contains a variable number of these two types of fibre. This proportion can be altered through use, to a certain extent, and this is especially important for musicians.

The connection between muscle and bone may be direct or, more typically, by means of a tendon ❹, a resistant and inextensible cord of white glossy fibres. In some areas the tendon is very large. This allows the muscle to perform at

> ## Musicians often ask
> **I had tendonitis in my right shoulder. A few days' rest managed to make the symptoms disappear but when I started playing again the pain came back. Do I have chronic tendonitis?** *One of the main reasons for inflammation of the shoulder tendons is that they are being rubbed because of a muscle imbalance. If we only remove the inflammation from the tendons but do not perform exercises to rebalance the muscles of the shoulder joint afterwards, the problem will reappear before too long as the act of playing rubs them again. So, in this case, we may not be talking about a chronic inflammation of the shoulder tendons but an unresolved imbalance. Your doctor or therapist will tell you if this is the case and how to correct it. If the problem proves to be playing-related, then systematic re-learning of the relevant movements will be necessary.*

a certain distance without the thickness of the muscle itself interfering or limiting movement. Due to their movements, tendons have few vessels and get very little blood flow. As blood is necessary for the healing process, if a tendon is injured or inflamed, it could take a long time to heal.

Protective covering ❺

The joints are protected by small sacs whose walls can secrete a fluid similar to that inside the joints. This fluid, along with the sacs' ability to stretch, makes it useful for avoiding friction between the structures it protects. For this reason it is found between the skin and bony protuberances (for example behind the elbow) or protecting tendons (for example, in the shoulder or the tendons in the hand).

Hypermobility: blessing or punishment?

The increased range of movements in one, some or all of the joints is a relatively frequent condition in musicians. It may be an asset for your hands or fingers if you are an instrumental musician but, although this is usually not serious, you may rather more easily suffer pain and inflammatory conditions in these areas. This is because you will, unconsciously, need to use greater muscular effort to stabilise these joints.

Hypermobility can partially disappear as you get older, but this will be less likely to happen if you continuously play using such joints in less than optimal positions. So, to avoid problems or to ensure that this will have no long-term effect on your career, you should:

1. use your joints in the optimum position (see *Chapter 3 – Posture. Your body in harmony with your instrument*) while playing and, also, when doing other repetitive manual tasks such as writing or typing on the computer keyboard;

2. train the muscles surrounding the hypermobile joints, especially those small ones contained in your hand. Hand-grip springs or weights are not recommended for musicians. Exercises must be specific for this condition so it is important that you should consult a hand therapist or an arts medicine advisor to assist you formulate the ones that will best suit you. You also can visit **www.institutart.com/handexercises**;

3. be patient. These little muscles in your hand will not get stronger and build up endurance with a few exercise routines. You need to perform the exercises regularly over a period of at least three months;

4. consider weight-relieving straps and supports and instrument modifications, to help to decrease loads on hypermobile joints (see *Chapter 4 – Musicians, instruments and the workplace*).

Your skeleton – some important areas

Shoulder and arm

Shoulder joint ❶

The joint between the humerus ❷ and the shoulder blade ❸ is one of the musician's most mobile joints. This is because the articular part of the humerus ❷ is a hemisphere, while the articular part of the shoulder blade ❸ is much smaller and practically flat and free from restrictions.

In order to avoid instability of the joint, this small socket between the humerus ❷ and the shoulder blade ❸ is compensated for by the balancing effect of the muscles surrounding it ❹, ❺ and ❻.

Connection to the trunk

With the exception of the weak support provided at the front by the collarbone ❼, the arm and the trunk are connected exclusively by muscles ❽ and ❾.

In addition to moving the shoulder blade ❸, this musculature fixes the arm to the trunk and allows the hand to move accurately. For this reason, any continuous activity requiring greater control or sustained pressure on the hand (such as playing an instrument or a singer holding a score) tends to strain and overload the stabilising musculature of the shoulder blade ❸.

Warning: Working with an instrument, like most everyday actions, tends to use the muscles that raise the arm ❺ and ❿ more than those that lower it ❻. This makes some muscles stronger than others and gradually causes the humerus ❷ to become offset at the point where it meets the shoulder blade ❸. This lifting (a) narrows the space for some shoulder tendons (b) and they may be compressed and rub (c), for instance, when the right arm of the flautist is raised to hold the instrument, when the bow of the violinist reaches the heel or a conductor's arm is raised to clearly mark an entrance to the orchestra.

Musicians often ask
Despite performing independent movements and strengthening exercises, why does the mobility of my fourth finger not improve a lot?
Continually working with an instrument increases the independent movements of the fingers. Even certain exercises away from the instrument can assist this. However, the anatomy of the muscles and tendons in the hand imposes certain unavoidable limits. Although these differ between musicians, the restricted movement of the fourth finger is the most marked, as it shares a common tendon, which then divides to activate each finger. In addition, its tendons are also intrinsically linked to its neighbouring fingers. Struggling too hard against these natural limits usually leads to the deterioration of the structures involved.

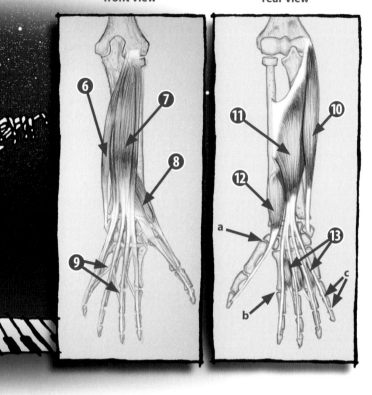

forearm and hand - front view

forearm and hand - rear view

Forearm and hand
Bones – ❶, ❷, ❸, ❹ and ❺

The radius ❶, through the actions of the muscles, can move around the ulna ❷ to turn the palm of the hand up or down. This crossed position of the bones is necessary, for instance, to place the hand on the keyboard and the continuous alternative rotation of the wrist ❸ is needed, for example, to produce slaps with the right-hand thumb on double-bass strings.

Although the bones of the wrist are bound tightly together by ligaments, they are able to move about between themselves and therefore allow for great mobility. They can move laterally (as when a percussionist taps on the snare drum), bend and extend (as when the pianist plays octaves) or rotate. Although keeping your wrist fixed will allow greater precision in the movements of your fingers when playing, it may not adapt well to some technical gestures.

But excessive mobility can overstress the joints or the tendons that run by the zone. For that reason you must find a way of avoiding excessive movements of the wrist whilst permitting it to contribute to the best position of the hand and the fingers on the instrument.

At the base of the hand, the joint of the wrist and metacarpals ❺ is very inflexible because their joint faces are cubic and not spherical in shape. This is extremely relevant for the second and third metacarpals whose rigidity gives them the necessary stability to produce fine finger movements. The fourth and fifth are a little more mobile and this allows you to close the palm of the hand while playing.

The thumb is different. Its articulation (**a**) allows it to move in all planes and to touch any other finger. This is necessary, for example, for the left thumb of clarinettists when they press the octave key.

66

In the same way, the metacarpals ❺ are spherical in shape where they join (**b**) the phalanges (fingers) ❹. This allows a certain degree of movement in all planes. However, where the phalangial joints ❹ meet each other their ends are rather flat (**c**). This only allows them to stretch (extension) and to bend (flexion).

Muscles of the posterior forearm – ❻, ❼, ❽

Many of the muscles that move the wrist and fingers are found on the back of the forearm. When the muscles that end in the wrist ❻ contract in isolation they cause the hand to move in the direction in which the muscle is pulling. But when they act together with the other muscles they produce extension of the wrist. There are also muscles that extend all the fingers at the same time ❼. In addition, the thumb, index and little fingers have their own muscles allowing them to move independently more easily ❽.

Tendinous bridges – ❾

To strengthen the hand and ensure that injury to, or rupture of, a tendon does not prevent finger extension, there are rigid links between the tendons ❾. These bridges vary between individuals as to their position, number and rigidity but they always exist. They cause the movement of a finger to be accompanied, to a greater or lesser degree, by the movement of the neighbouring fingers or, if these remain still, they restrict the amount of their mobility.

Muscles of the anterior forearm – ❿ and ⓫

As with the muscles of the posterior forearm, because of the long tendons that are attached to the wrist, the muscles of the musician's anterior forearm move (if one acts in isolation) or flex the wrist (if they act together) ❿. Other muscles, which also have long tendons, reach the fingertips and produce simultaneous flexion of all the fingers together ⓫.

Muscles of the hand – ⓬ and ⓭

There are some small muscles in the hand, which contribute to the mobility of the fingers. Some belong to individual

fingers. For example, the thumb has muscles that allow it to flex, move towards or move away from the middle finger or make a pincer movement with the other fingers ⓬. Others work together with the tendons of the forearm muscles ⓭. They allow movements with greater freedom, and more harmonious positions and actions.

Tendon sheaths – ⓮

At all the points where a tendon changes direction or where it is necessary that it is kept close to the bone, there is a type of tunnel, or fibrous tube ⓮ which guides its passage. To minimise rubbing, the tendon has a protective covering made by lubricated tissue (see page 63). This allows for smooth movement. The tunnels are relatively rigid and perfectly match the thickness of the tendon. This means that the tendon rubs more if the position of the joint is forced. In this situation, especially if the movement is repetitive, the protective sheath or the tendon itself, or both, may become inflamed and swollen (causing tenosinovitis and trigger finger), making the tendon movement more difficult and painful. Keeping the joints in the correct position will avoid this rubbing (see *Chapter 3 – Posture*).

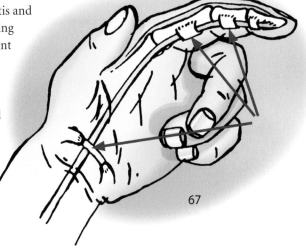

Spinal column

The spine comprises 29 very similar bones called vertebrae. The principal parts of a vertebra are:

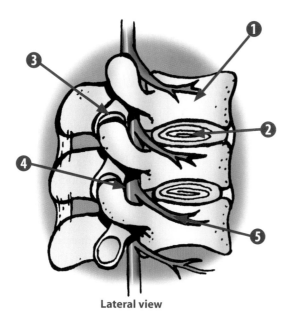

Lateral view

Vertebral body ❶
The most forward facing part of each vertebra is like a cylinder and the majority of the body's weight is transmitted through it.

Vertebral disc ❷
Special cartilage situated between the bodies ❶ of the vertebrae, allowing movement between them and cushioning impacts.

Posterior joints ❸
In addition to the disc joint ❷, the vertebrae are interconnected by small joints that stabilise the movements of the spine. They can only slide smoothly if they are correctly aligned. Poor posture and muscle imbalances may mean that they do not work properly, causing pain and restricting mobility.

Spinal cord ❹
In addition to being the body's weight-bearing axis, one of the functions of the spinal column is to protect the spinal cord. This is a collection of nerve fibres that runs through the channel formed by the vertebrae just behind the vertebral body ❶. Its function is to connect the brain with the rest of the body and to generate reflex movements.

Nerve roots ❺
Nerve fibres branch out from the spinal cord ❹ through the small spaces on either side between the vertebrae. These roots form nerves that transmit sensations and commands to move muscles. This space is in direct contact with the disc ❷ and with the posterior joint ❸, so any disturbance or inflammation in this area will quickly irritate the root. This will cause weakness and/or a change in sensation (pain, numbness, pins and needles, and so on) in the area governed by that root. In the same way, sustaining a twisted neck position – for example, playing the flute or to visually control your left-hand movements on the cello – can narrow the exit space of the nerve roots and irritate them.

Musicians often ask
If, when playing, I keep my head bowed towards the side of the violin for some time, I get a painful numbness in my fingers that forces me to stop. Could I have a disc problem?
Although the only way to discover the exact origin of such symptoms is a detailed study of each case, an injury to the vertebral disc is not the sole or even the most frequent cause of these problems in a musician. Excessive muscle tension possibly combined with a forced posture of the spine may compress or narrow the path of the nerves running from the spine to the arm at neck height and produce these symptoms in the hand. The same symptoms can even be produced by an over-flexed elbow or wrist.

Alignment

The vertebrae are arranged in such a way that, seen from the front or the rear, they form a completely straight column. The upper part, formed by 7 cervical vertebrae **6** is very mobile. The central part, made up of 12 thoracic vertebrae **7** has little mobility. The ribs are attached to this part. The five lumbar vertebrae **8** are the strongest since the body's load is focused on this area. The last five vertebrae, the sacrum **9**, are fused together and form part of the pelvis.

If we look at the spine from the side we can see a series of curves. Not only are these natural, they are essential for improved resistance to loads and correct operation.

Lateral View

To maintain correct alignment, a balance between the muscles situated on either side of the spine **10** and between the spine and the muscles situated in front (the abdominals) is essential. Our bodies are constructed on symmetrical principles and rely on this equality of balance to maintain healthy posture. Any asymmetrical activity or posture (playing the violin, carrying your instrument or equipment, for example) means a greater load on one side and a degree of twisting of the spine leading to greater work for the muscles on that side (see *Chapter 3 – Posture*).

Basic connections

Once the nerve roots leave the spinal column they form the different nerves. In the cervical area the nerves are responsible for transmitting movement commands to the muscles of the upper extremities and for communicating sensations from there back to the brain.

Nerves are relatively sensitive to pressure and stretching and therefore pass through areas protected by the bones and muscles.

Weak points

However, during their passage, there are certain areas where the nerves are more vulnerable for a musician.

In the neck ❶

In order to exit the spinal column the nerve must pass through the tiny space between two vertebrae and between the muscles in the side of the neck. Muscle tension, poor posture or direct pressure from certain instruments resting on this area (for example violin, viola, thin straps of wind instruments or accordion) may irritate the nerves causing symptoms in the shoulder, arm or hand, although the problem is really in the neck.

The elbow ❷

The ulnar nerve is easily irritated at the elbow, either when the joint is kept in an extremely flexed position or when it is rested on an edge or hard area. This could happen, for example, if the guitar neck is placed too low, or you are too close to the keyboard. It can also happen if you play the piccolo instead of the flute (since this will result in a more flexed position of your elbow) or if you rest your arm on the corner of an armrest or table. It is quite common for the ulnar nerve to be very near the surface, and in this case the nerve will be more vulnerable. Irritation of the ulnar nerve usually leads to symptoms along the inside of the forearm, and in the ring and little fingers.

The wrist ❸

In this area the median nerve and the ulnar nerve pass below thick ligaments (the carpal and Guyon tunnels) and between the tendons leading to the fingers. Forced postures of the wrist, tendon inflammation or thickening of these ligaments will lead to discomfort (tingling, pins and needles, numbness, etc.) or, if left untreated, possible weakness in the hand and fingers.

The fingers ❹

Those instruments that rest on the sides of the fingers (for example, the flute) may irritate the nerve endings.

70

Your respiratory system – basic information

In order to breathe and produce sound, we use structures that form part of what is known as the respiratory system. Understanding breathing is, of course, vitally important for wind players and singers, but is also far more important to, for instance, string players, keyboardists or percussionists than they may realise. Good breathing habits will improve oxygenation and posture and can relieve tension. Its basic components are as follows.

Mucous membrane ❶
The conduits and cavities of the respiratory system are covered with a mucous membrane that warms and moistens the air and filters out unwanted particles and micro-organisms. To do this, the membrane produces viscous mucous containing protective substances that trap and neutralise the particles. To avoid the build up of mucous and particles, it also has filaments that move in a synchronised way, acting as a conveyor belt to push the mucous and particles stuck in them out of the respiratory tract.

Salivary glands ❷
These are the organs that produce and secrete saliva in the mouth. Saliva is principally produced when stimulated by chewing food, but also from contact with the tongue moving around the mouth. We produce on average a litre of saliva every day. It helps to keep the oral cavity moist and clean, contributes to good dental health and digestion, and assists swallowing and making sounds. Nervous stimuli also play a part in controlling the flow of saliva and may leave the mouth completely dry in stressful situations such as exams or concerts or, on other occasions, can flood it unnecessarily.

Lungs ❸
Similar in appearance to a sponge, our two lungs are situated in the thoracic cavity (formed by the ribs, the sternum and the spine). Each lung is covered by a thin layer of protective tissue called the pleura.

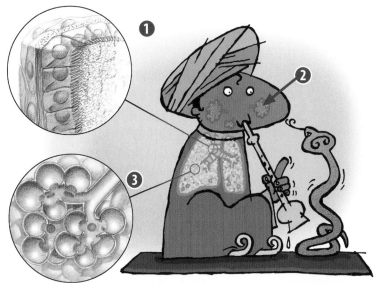

Musicians often ask
When I take a tranquilliser before a performance I notice that my mouth is very dry, which has a negative effect on my interpretative abilities. Is there a way to avoid this? *Saliva production may be affected by many causes, including taking certain drugs. Although it is not always the case, some tranquillisers and medicines to treat allergies, nausea and vomiting, and amphetamines, may inhibit the secretion of saliva. The only way to prevent this is to seek alternative solutions avoiding the use of tranquillisers (see Chapter 6 – Mind and music).*

The principal function of the lungs is to exchange gases between the blood and the air outside (oxygen, carbon dioxide, etc.). However, their ability to take in (inspiration) and expel (expiration) air using the respiratory tract also provides the bellows that vibrate the vocal folds and, for wind instruments, the reed or lips.

The architecture of the lungs could be compared to that of a tree where the trunk and branches are hollow allowing the air to circulate through their interior. The leaves would be small, flexible balloons, which inflate or deflate as air enters or exits.

Your sound production and modulation system

Just below the facial skin there is a delicate musculature whose basic function is to open and close the mouth and eyes and form facial expressions. None of these functions requires very powerful muscles. Moreover, large muscles would make this task difficult. This is why the so-called mimic muscles of the face comprise fine, delicate strands of fibres.

Unlike the other muscles of the body, these muscles do not start at or connect directly to the bone. Although some of them do have a strong point of attachment, the majority are attached to the skin or to other muscles forming a kind of network of muscles.

This network of muscles meets at the orbicular muscle of the lips ❶, which runs round the mouth orifice and causes the furrowing of the lips.

However, musicians (for example, trumpet and bassoon players) are not seeking lip furrowing but tension. For this, it is essential that the muscles connected to the orbicular ❶ also contract: the mentalis ❷, risorius ❸, zygomaticus ❹ and buccinator ❺. This contraction must be coordinated and as symmetrical as possible to achieve maximum efficiency and avoid injuries.

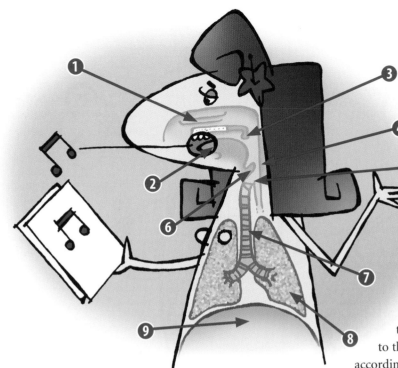

Nostrils ❶

These constitute the entry point for air into the respiratory system. They help to condition the air. As the entrance is relatively narrow, when you need to inhale a large amount of air quickly, you normally use the mouth. This prevents the nostrils from warming, humidifying and cleaning the air and could cause dryness, irritation and infection of the respiratory tract.

Tongue ❷

This is a muscular organ that is used, on the one hand, to identify taste, condition and swallowing of food and, on the other, for speaking, singing and producing and modulating the sound of wind instruments.

Unlike the other muscles of the body, its fibres are arranged in three different planes. This, together with the fact that other muscles connect at the front and back, gives it unique movement: it is the only muscle that can lengthen by contracting its fibres (it does this by activating the vertical and transversal fibres simultaneously). Its surface is covered with mucous tissue.

Soft palate ❸

Unlike the rest of the palate, which has a rigid base of bone as a support, the posterior part of the roof of the mouth is fibro-muscular. This allows it to move, in conjunction with its small appendix (the uvula). Its basic action is to close the connecting passage to the nose using its muscular fibres. This allows wind instrumentalists (for instance, saxophone or horn players) and singers to direct all the air coming from the lungs to the mouth and avoid escape of pressure to the nose. The degree of closure may also vary according to the desired sound when speaking or singing (for instance when producing the sound 'dong' or singing with a closed mouth).

Pharynx ❹

This is a shared channel for the passage of air and food, which connects the posterior part of the nasal cavity, mouth and larynx. It is formed by constrictive muscles (these close the aperture of the pharynx when they contract), which assist the movement of food towards the oesophagus. The same muscles allow the pharynx to change its size, altering the tone of the voice. An excessive constrictive action however, will not assist singers to project their voices easily and in a relaxed fashion or control the sound of wind instruments.

The Eustachian tube (see page 76) enters at the top of the pharynx.

Larynx ❺

This is the part of the vocal apparatus, which vibrates in response to air flow. It comprises different cartilaginous tissue and muscles and is lined with mucous membrane. It also acts as a triple-stop valve – comprising the epiglottis ❻, the ventricular folds and the ventricles (see page 75 for

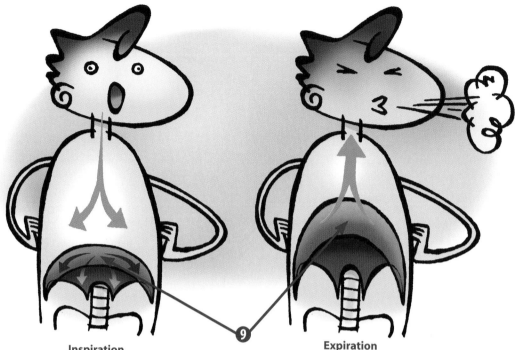

Inspiration | **Expiration**

more detail) – that prevents food or foreign bodies entering the lungs.

Trachea ❼

This is a respiratory channel connecting the larynx with the lungs. It comprises several rings of cartilage that prevent its walls from collapsing. It divides into two bronchi, which are in turn also subdivided into smaller and smaller tubes until the lung tissue is reached.

Lungs ❽

See the explanation on page 71.

Diaphragm ❾

This separates the thoracic cavity from the abdomen and is the principal muscle responsible for inhaling air into the lungs (inspiration). It is dome-shaped and its base is attached to the lower ribs, the sternum and the lumbar region (some people say it resembles a parachute). As it contracts it moves outwards, causing inspiration. When it relaxes it recovers its dome shape and air is passively expelled from the lungs (expiration).

74

Musicians often ask
How should I work the diaphragm to expel air more powerfully? *Apart from the tongue that, as it has muscle fibres arranged in different directions, can lengthen and contract itself, muscles can only contract. Once contracted, only the opposing muscles or the elasticity of the area can return them to their initial relaxed position. In the case of the diaphragm, this means that its contraction causes the intake of air into the lungs and its relaxation, because of the flexibility of the structures of the thorax (as if it were a balloon) returns it to its initial condition, expelling the air. If you want to accelerate this process of expiration, it is necessary to use and strengthen other muscles such as the abdominals. Contracting these when combined with the relaxation of the diaphragm assists what we call active expiration.*

Front view

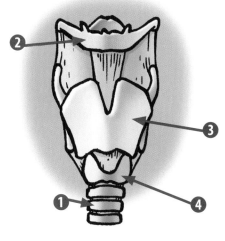

Superior view

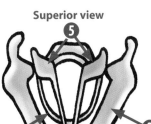

Cartilages

Muscles

Mucous tissue

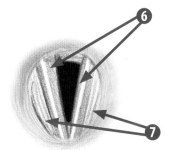

Larynx

Both singers and wind instrumentalists use the larynx, whether to produce sound (see page 18) or to regulate the flow of air (see page 21).

As with the trachea **1** (see 74), the larynx has cartilaginous tissue that prevents it from collapsing. But it also has other features that allow it to change its volume and shape.

Hyoid bone **2**

This is the only bone in the body that is not connected to any other bone. Via muscles, ligaments and membranes it helps to keep the larynx in the correct position at all times.

Thyroid cartilage **3**

This is the largest cartilage in the larynx, known as the Adam's apple, and it supports most of the tissues in the larynx. Its size and shape vary with age and according to gender. It determines, to a great extent, the voice's characteristics.

Cricoid cartilage **4**

This is a ring-shaped cartilage that supports most of the vocal folds' structures.

Arytenoids cartilages **5**

These are two cartilages that are joined to the posterior part of the cricoid cartilage **4** and support the vocal folds. Their small size allows rapid position changes (tilting).

Vocal folds (vocal cords) **6**

These folds located on either side of the larynx comprise mucous tissue, ligaments and the vocal muscle. The movements of the thyroid cartilage **3** change their length while those of the arytenoid cartilage **5** bring them together, closing the space between the vocal folds (called the glottis).

Ventricular folds or bands (false vocal cords) **7**

On either side of the internal surface of the larynx there are two folds of mucous tissue which house muscles that help the larynx to close. They are located just above the vocal folds **6**. Their function is uniquely one of protection (during vomiting, coughing, etc.) and they have no role in making sounds.

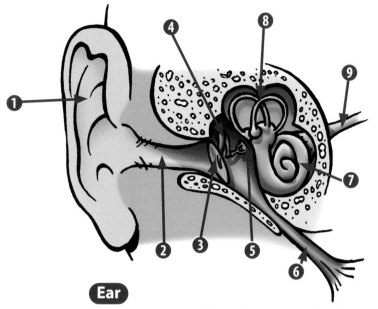

Ear

The ear is usually described as being divided into three parts: the outer ear, middle ear and inner ear.

Outer ear

The role of the outer ear is to conduct sound towards the middle ear and it comprises the following:

Ear ❶

This is made up of skin-covered cartilage that, in a bell-like fashion, gathers sound waves and channels them towards the auditory canal ❷.

Auditory canal ❷

This is an air-filled cavity leading to the ear drum ❸. It has hairy formations and wax secreted by glands in the covering skin to protect against the entry of foreign objects.

Middle ear

The role of the middle ear is to channel sound from the outer to the inner ear.

Eardrum ❸

This membrane is attached to the auditory canal ❷ by means of a fibrous ring very similar to a drum skin. Its function is to transmit sound waves travelling through the air to the interior of the middle ear, transforming them into mechanical vibrations.

Auditory bones ❹

The next part of the middle ear is made up of three bones – the hammer (*malleus*), anvil (*incus*) and stirrups (*stapes*) – which are situated in a row and form an articulated chain. The hammer is connected to the eardrum and the stirrups to the membrane of the *fenestra ovalis* ❺. The anvil is situated between the two. Ligaments and muscles support this chain of bones. The action of these muscles reduces vibrations, cushioning extremely loud noises if necessary.

Eustachian tube ❻

The role of this mucous-lined channel connecting the middle ear with the pharynx is to adjust the pressure of the middle ear to that of the outer ear to allow correct vibration and sound transmission. For example, when atmospheric pressure alters because of a change in altitude, the movements of the pharynx, especially the act of swallowing, open its aperture, which allows air to move in one direction or another. The balance of pressures is re-established and hearing returns to normal.

Inner ear

The inner ear is located entirely within the bone of the skull and houses the hearing and balance sensors.

Cochlea ❼

This is a spiral bony conduit, sometimes called the snail on account of its appearance, whose interior contains several canals filled with fluid and covered by cells with delicate hairlike expansions. Vibrations reaching the *fenestra ovalis* ❺ are transmitted to the fluid, which in turn moves these 'hairs', stimulating the cells. This stimulates the auditory nerve ❾, which transmits the auditory information to the brain.

Semicircular canals ❽

The semicircular canals comprise the organ responsible for the sense of balance and rotation. There are three semicircular canals each of which is directed in one of the three planes of movement. The organ's role is to detect movements of the head and pass this information to the brain. Each canal is full of a fluid containing small calcium crystals that stimulate the receptor cells of the canals when they move.

Quiz

1. **Hypermobility could become a health problem in a musician because:**
   a) it reduces joint lubrication;
   b) it needs supplementary muscular effort;
   c) it damages the bone.

2. **A muscle is:**
   a) a group of thick (slow movement) and thin (fast movement) contractile fibres;
   b) a tissue formed by thousands of tendons;
   c) a tendon that can be voluntarily contracted.

3. **Shoulder tendon inflammation could easily return due to:**
   a) the stability of the shoulder joint;
   b) unresolved muscular imbalance;
   c) increased space for the shoulder tendons.

4. **The second and third fingers allow better fine movements than the other fingers because:**
   a) they are larger;
   b) their muscles are more precise;
   c) their joints with the wrist bones are very inflexible.

5. **The muscles of the forearm basically affect:**
   a) fingers and wrist;
   b) only the thumb, index and little fingers;
   c) only the wrist.

6. **Some fingers are difficult to move separately because:**
   a) they don't have their own muscles;
   b) they have tendinous bridges between them;
   c) answers a and b are correct.

7. **Which is the best way to prevent the inflammation of tendons at the point where they go through tunnels ?**
   a) Repeat the movement enough times to increase tendon resistance and lubrication.
   b) Maintain a correct joint position to avoid tendon rubbing.
   c) Stretch the tunnels.

8. **With reference to the spinal column, it is true that:**
   a) the discs only exist in the lower part of the spinal column, where the loads are greater;
   b) correct spinal alignment is maintained by muscle balance;
   c) the spinal column can easily tolerate asymmetrical activities or postures due to the stability of the posterior joints.

9. Nerves can be damaged by:
   a) poor posture or direct pressure from certain instruments;
   b) sustained or repeated extreme positions of a joint;
   c) answers a and b are correct.

10. With reference to the respiratory system, it is false that:
   a) its mucous membrane filters, warms and moistens the air;
   b) the secretion of saliva can be instigated by nervous stimuli;
   c) the structure of the lungs is similar to that of a tree.

11. You cannot be fully aware of the working of your facial muscles because they:
   a) work together as a network;
   b) don't have sensors;
   c) are fine strands of fibres.

12. The larynx:
   a) is the part of the vocal apparatus that causes vibration;
   b) is a shared channel for the passage of air and food;
   c) collapses during inspiration.

13. The diaphragm:
   a) is the principal muscle for exhaling air;
   b) is in the pelvis;
   c) resembles a parachute.

14. Sound vibrations stimulate the auditory nerve by:
   a) balancing the pressures between the mouth and the ear;
   b) transmitting the vibrations at the *fenestra ovalis* to the fluid of the cochlea;
   c) moving the small calcium crystals contained in the semicircular canals.

Question	Correct answer	If your answer is wrong, please read the page again and find out why you made your mistake
1	b	see page 64
2	a	see page 63
3	b	see page 65
4	c	see page 66
5	a	see page 67
6	c	see page 67
7	b	see page 67
8	b	see page 69
9	c	see page 69
10	c	see page 71
11	b	see page 72
12	a	see page 73
13	c	see page 74
14	b	see page 76

Chapter 6

Mind and music
Further psychological aspects

No one fully understands yet what the essential ingredients are that go to make up a successful musical performance. What we do know is that, in addition to purely technical and physical aspects, psychological factors such as personality, character or state of mind play a very important role.

In Chapter 1 (*Basic functions*) we reviewed some aspects such as memorisation, learning strategies or mental practice that could be considered as relevant psychological processes in musicians. In this chapter we will analyse others such as anxiety, relaxation and visualisation.

It is even possible that the type of instrument you chose or agreed to play when you were young may have had a significant impact on the development of your personality, your way of playing and, in some cases, the emergence of psychological conflicts. So, for example, we might agree that while a piano may be seen as part of the furniture in a home and is, therefore, of some value to all the family, the majority of other instruments have a very limited impact on the family and possess greater personal value. There are some instruments, such as the guitar, viola, harmonica or sax, that you can carry with you. Although you can play them when you are alone, in different ways they encourage you to seek out colleagues so that you can grow as a musician. We could say that these instruments facilitate socialisation. It is thought by anthropologists that music is a socially driven phenomenon, and its obvious power on us and also its therapeutic value can, in some ways, be ascribed to this. However, you could study the piano by yourself all your life without needing to be accompanied by anyone – which could be seen as an invitation to loneliness.

The working conditions of professional musicians and also of full-time music students also create a context in which they are more susceptible to experiencing and communicating psychological changes and in which psychological disorders are more likely to develop. The high level of competitiveness, the degree of perfectionism required, the constant scrutiny of the public, precarious employment, professional uncertainty, changes in timetable, problematic interpersonal relationships in orchestras or sudden changes in habits are just some of the causes.

Injuries or the fear of being unable to work at maximum ability are also a huge cause of stress for musicians, mainly for those who have been on stage since they were young and whose self-esteem depends, to a large degree, on public acclaim. As a result, musicians have a higher proportion of episodes of depression and anxiety or sleep disturbance than most other professionals.

Although you may be unable to control or modify some of these factors, it is possible to achieve greater self-control, which will enable you to avoid future problems and make performing a more pleasant and efficient experience.

Anxiety: friend and foe

Pau Casals used to say that before going on stage the true artist undergoes a small degree of illness that, fortunately, is cured immediately by contact with the public.

In fact, many musicians maintain that, in order for their performance to have 'electricity', their body must be in a state of some nervous tension. This increases their level of motivation, sensitivity and imagination. In other words, not only is a small amount of anxiety normal, it also appears necessary for some musicians' efficiency.

But, more often than is desirable, this anxiety is overwhelming and you cannot control it; it interferes with and has a negative impact on your performance. In such instances we are talking about performance anxiety, a common problem for both amateur and professional musicians.

It is believed that for the majority of musicians the relationship between the level of arousal or nervous tension and performance follows a rainbow-shaped curve. Initially, performance improves as nervous arousal increases. However, if this increases beyond a certain level, annoying symptoms and pessimistic thoughts start to appear and have a negative impact on performance. There is even a point where, particularly because of cognitive anxiety (negative thoughts), performing ability falls catastrophically.

According to this response model, it seems clear that your objective is to achieve a certain degree of nervous arousal but to keep it in the first part of the curve. If necessary, relaxation and anxiety control techniques (see later on in this chapter) can help you to do this.

How performance anxiety manifests itself

Performance anxiety, also called stage fright, is an exaggerated fear, often incapacitating, of playing in public caused by the activation of an emergency response. It is a set of reactions occurring involuntarily as a preparatory mechanism for dangerous situations where your body must 'fight or flee'. It's a mechanism that your most distant ancestors already possessed, and it gave them more survival options in the jungle or when going out to hunt mammoths. It might be helpful to you when you are driving and a child suddenly steps out into the road. The immediate release of adrenaline into your blood makes it more likely that you will be able to respond to the incident in an effective manner. But that's not much use to you as a musician – unless you're planning to run off stage or attack the public!

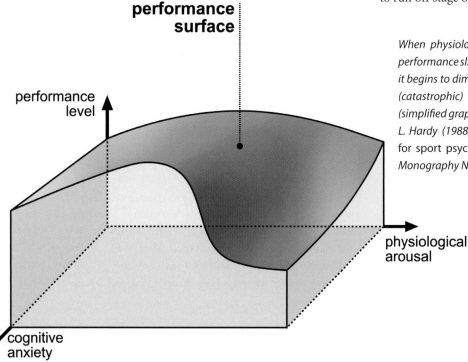

performance surface

performance level

cognitive anxiety

physiological arousal

When physiological arousal and cognitive anxiety increase, performance slightly improves; however, beyond a certain point it begins to diminish. This reduction is much more pronounced (catastrophic) when cognitive anxiety increases significantly (simplified graphic of the catastrophic model, from J. Fazey and L. Hardy (1988), The inverted-U hypothesis: A catastrophe for sport psychology. *British Association for Sports Sciences Monography No. 1, Leeds: National Coaching Foundation).*

So what you feel is an increase in the force with which the heart contracts. This is originally designed to make more blood reach the muscles so that you can run or fight more powerfully. But now you are feeling it as discomfort and worrying palpitations in your chest. You will also feel the increase in lung activity and the expansion of the respiratory channels to allow more oxygen to enter the blood as a sensation of breathlessness. Blood being sent to the muscles leaves the digestive system with less blood, which causes the sensation of 'butterflies' in your stomach. The redirection of all fluids to the circulation to make more blood available leaves the mouth dry, and activation of the body's heating system causes the hands and forehead to perspire.

All of these responses give you more opportunities to survive if you find yourself facing a hungry lion. But they are much less useful if you are in front of an audience that is expecting you to entertain them.

Normally, in addition to these physical symptoms, there are cognitive manifestations of anxiety in the form of images or thoughts or of messages you give to yourself. These include fear of making mistakes and feelings of inadequacy and worrying about things happening. It also interferes with judgement so that you are less likely to make sensible, rational decisions or to appraise what is going on realistically ('I think I am going to faint', 'I'm almost sure to make a dreadful mistake and that will ruin everything', 'I wasn't up to it', 'Everyone noticed how nervous I was', 'I made a fool of myself', 'Why did I play if I wasn't ready to?').

The symptoms are not always obvious. In some cases the problem becomes apparent because of the fact that you are not fully enjoying what you are doing. In fact, you are concentrating more on avoiding making mistakes than on enjoying and communicating all your hard work. When you stop playing you experience a pleasant feeling but more because you've stopped playing than because you've savoured the moment. At these times we are also confronted by performance anxiety.

> ## Musicians often ask
> **What sets this reaction off in my body and why can't I control it? Do I have some mental illness or problem?** *This is nothing unusual. The only problem is that a response is being triggered at a time when it is not helpful for you. It's a response that is learned unintentionally and that therefore can be unlearned with appropriate training.*

> # Important: Unless you are seriously ill, although it is an unpleasant experience, acute anxiety cannot harm you. Anxiety is not dangerous for the body and you should remember that you will always recover from it.

Performance anxiety often shows itself minutes, hours or even many days before a performance as worry, insomnia, irritability, digestive problems, or a lack of vitality or emotional instability.

As a general rule these symptoms usually improve with age and experience but many musicians live with them all their lives.

Why it happens

Although it is customary to think that the problem starts with a past event that particularly left its mark on you (a situation where you made a fool of yourself, where you were strongly criticised, where you had a really bad time), it is not usually possible to detect what this event was. What usually happens is that it develops as the result of a combination of different factors.

It occurs most often when you have practised too much or too little, when you are scared of getting injured, when the expectations surrounding you are high or when you are genetically predisposed to it.

Some personality traits are also linked to performance anxiety. One is perfectionism, especially when it is motivated by environmental rather than personal reasons. This tends to raise your expectations about yourself and others. You analyse your mistakes in depth but not the things you got right. You are very critical of yourself and suffer from low self-esteem. Another trait is a tendency to have an excessive need for self-control, which makes you uncomfortable and unable to succeed in unpredictable circumstances. The way you were brought up also affects you. Some parents unconsciously cause their children, often through imitation, to avoid exposing themselves to certain social situations and encourage their fear of looking ridiculous or of looking bad in front of others by exaggerating the negative consequences.

Musicians are often encouraged (by teachers, parents or by themselves) to take examinations or appear in public before they are completely ready or before they have developed an adequate safety margin to do this. In this way the exam or performance becomes an event that causes anxiety instead of an enjoyable experience. The margin becomes even narrower when irrational ideas of perfection have been instilled that make failure unacceptable, especially in front of others. The feeling of being under threat increases when the probability or seriousness of a feared event is overestimated, when what you or others can do to improve the situation is undervalued, and the more you play alone (playing solo creates more fear than playing in a duet, a duet more than a trio, an so on).

These factors can easily affect the way you react when playing and as a result your performance suffers and anxiety increases. One bad experience of performing leads to another; the experience becomes internalised through a process of conditioning and so the fear is reproduced in later situations. Anxiety becomes a response to something that might happen and not a response to something that does happen. A vicious circle is created whereby the way mistakes are perceived leads to an increase in anxiety and this anxiety makes it much more likely that mistakes will be made.

Moreover, anxiety can affect your self-reflective capacity. This, in turn, may influence self-esteem and faith in one's ability, which may also increase the anxiety felt, and increases the likelihood of pathological anxiety developing.

Finally, contrary to how it may appear, when you avoid the stress-inducing situation and thereby gain some relief, you increase the likelihood of the anxiety occurring again. This is known as negative reinforcement. This is similar to avoidance, where you avoid contact with the source of anxiety (not turning up at an audition, cancelling a concert, and so on) and escape, where you do confront your fear but do something to avoid the symptoms (not looking at the public, wearing a lucky charm, taking a tranquilliser or consuming alcohol, thinking that the performance is unimportant and that it doesn't matter if you make a bad job of it...).

All musicians must take these factors into account and resolve the issues that they can before anxiety sets in. Perhaps the most effective form of prevention lies in the hands of the teacher who is responsible for the beginner musician. Music should be considered to be an art and a pleasure, not a competition or technical perfection to be achieved within a given period of time, as this creates a tense atmosphere which obstructs our enjoyment in performing, turning what should be an experience of playing into one of merely working.

What can you do?

Many musicians experience stage fright and others experience psychological disturbances without realising it – it is their colleagues or relatives who point it out to them. Others do accept that they have a problem but refuse to consult a professional in the field. They believe that they can solve the problem, that they have to be strong and that nobody knows them better than they know themselves. So, the first step to cope with the problem is to accept it, to understand that it can be solved and that, therefore, it makes no sense to live with it and that you have to seek the help you need. But you shouldn't wait until you have a real problem before deciding to use techniques or strategies that may help to make performing more enjoyable and productive.

Each musician will need different techniques according to her or his make-up and nature. Below we discuss some of the techniques that have been demonstrated to be most effective for musicians working to adjust their degree of stress to desirable levels. Try to find which match your needs best.

General aspects

Lifestyle is immensely important in managing stress. Taking regular physical exercise (see *Chapter 7 – Troubleshooting for musicians*) will also improve performance when playing and will avoid fluctuations in performance. You have to remember that family, economic and health factors play a significant role in your state of mind and you should be aware of how they can affect your performance.

Diet also plays an important role. Before a concert, taking easily digestible meals with complex carbohydrates (rice, bread or pasta, fruit and vegetables) and avoiding high amounts of caffeine and spicy foods may help to calm stage fright. Certain foods, such as bananas, are also popularly believed to have a sedative effect.

It is also very useful to establish routines of behaviour before a concert in order to put yourself in the best mental and physical state for performing. These routines could also include planning meals and drinks on the day of the performance, a short nap, positive self-talk (see page 87), a focus on performance goals and relaxation strategies (see page 85), wearing comfortable clothes, arriving at the workplace in good time in order to check that everything is just right, and warm-up exercises (see page 93) before you play.

Active substances

Many musicians try substances at their own initiative that they think may reduce their anxiety such as alcohol, cannabis or diazepam (Valium®). Although their use may relieve some of the symptoms, they can be destructive as they create dependency and, to a certain extent, alter the performance. Beta-blockers, such as propanolol (Inderal® and Sumial® are the most used trade names), are more suitable as they eliminate many of the physical symptoms of anxiety but leave the head clear. However, they cannot be considered an ideal group of medicines as they may cause side-effects such as impotency, diarrhoea, insomnia, rashes, dryness of the eyes, nausea and tiredness. They are particularly dangerous for people who suffer from asthma, diabetes or changes in the heart's electrical activity. For these reasons we strongly advise that they should not be used without the consent of both your student health adviser and your doctor.

Although these medications may be useful in special situations or when other treatments are not effective, psychological procedures aimed at restoring self-control are the most preferable treatment as they use the musician's own resources.

Working on the physiological response

Many psychologists believe that, in order to resolve performance anxiety, it is fundamental to expose yourself repeatedly to the situations you fear until your anxiety disappears. Clearly, this cannot be done at random. You have to find a way for the body to adapt and respond appropriately to the problem. The following methods are commonly used.

Progressive exposure

When anxiety appears, it does not occur in a stable way. At the beginning it gradually increases, but after 30–40 minutes, it starts to reduce until after an hour and a half to two hours it disappears altogether. According to this principle of exhausting response – and considering that anxiety is not dangerous and cannot harm you, and that you will always recover from the anxiety – you have to expose yourself gradually to different situations of increasing stress in order to adapt to it.

How to carry out progressive exposure

Make a list of up to ten situations that make you anxious. Arrange them in order of least to most troublesome (for example the first on the list could be 'playing alone in my bedroom' and the last 'performing a solo in a concert hall'). Although it may be difficult to reproduce some of the situations on your list exactly (for example, 'playing in a concert hall with only my friends in the audience'), try to find a way of reproducing them, if only approximately.

You must confront the first on the list and carry on playing in this situation until, after a period of time that will vary, the anxiety reduces and you have spent 15 or 20 minutes playing at this low level of anxiety (it does not have to be completely free of anxiety). Repeat the exposure to that situation for some days so that you get used to it and your body does not respond with anxiety. Usually, as you repeat the exposure, the maximum level of anxiety diminishes and the time it takes you to achieve a low level of nervousness reduces. Move on to the next situation when on a minimum of three occasions you have experienced no or very low anxiety, and in this way slowly work your way through your list.

Relaxation

Regularly practising relaxation techniques helps to reduce the body's response to stress, prevents its cumulative effects, improves memory and concentration, increases performance, and decreases muscle tension. Relaxation can be practised regularly or as part of a routine of exercises prior to performing. There are many relaxation strategies that have been shown to be helpful for musicians. These include, for example, progressive muscle relaxation, mental suggestions and imagery to produce a relaxed state, meditation, breathing awareness, yoga, tai chi and stretching.

Progressive Muscular Relaxation (PMR)

This technique allows you to practise relaxation by comparing relaxed and tense states.

To begin:

- Choose a quiet place, alone, with no distractions, not even background music. When you are used to the technique, you will be able to perform it in any situation and environment.

- Remove anything that may get in your way (such as shoes and jewellery) and wear loose clothing.

- It is preferable to practise before meals to avoid interfering with your digestion.

- Sit in a comfortable chair with your arms and legs uncrossed. Although you can practise lying down on a bed, it is better not to do this if you tend to fall asleep.

- Practise some deep breathing (see page 14) before you start and continue it throughout the exercise.

- Some people experience a sudden fall in their blood pressure when they get up quickly, which could cause them to faint. Therefore, at the end of the session, remain relaxed with your eyes closed for a few seconds and then get up slowly.

Important: Although this is a very gentle technique, if you have previously had serious injuries or illnesses you should consult your doctor about whether there are any particular risks for you before practising PMR, as intense muscle tensing could aggravate some pre-existing injuries.

First objective: to master relaxation

Step one: Tension

Select a muscle group according to the sequence suggested in the table of muscle groups. Concentrate on this muscle group. Inhale slowly and squeeze the muscles as hard as you can for about eight seconds. If you are working with the hand make a tight fist. If you are working with the face muscles you could grimace, close your eyes as tightly as possible, clench your teeth, and even move your ears up if you can.

Although in the beginning it will be difficult to achieve this, and you should not feel inept because of it, you should try not to tense other muscle groups apart from the muscles you are working. Remember that one of the objectives of the training is also to enable you to isolate some muscles from others. If you are tensing the hand, concentrate on not tensing the arm or shoulder. With practice you will learn to make very fine distinctions between muscles.

Anyway, remember that there is no part of your body that can be completely isolated from the rest. On page 66 you can see how, for example, many hand movements are produced by the muscles of the forearm. So when you tense your hand there will always be a certain amount of unavoidable tension in the forearm.

It is important that you experience a high degree of tension or even moderate pain at some moments. But take care not to hurt yourself.

Muscle groups

● Right foot	● Entire right arm
● Right lower leg and foot	● Left hand
● Entire right leg	● Left forearm and hand
● Left foot	● Entire left arm
● Left lower leg and foot	● Abdomen
● Entire left leg	● Chest
● Right hand	● Neck and shoulders
● Right forearm and hand	● Face

If you are left-handed, you may prefer to start with your left side.

Step two: Releasing the tension

After holding the tension for eight seconds, gradually release it while exhaling. It is very important that you notice the difference between tension and relaxation. Stay relaxed for about 15 seconds and then repeat the tension/relaxation cycle. You'll probably notice more sensations the second time. As this happens, you should try to reduce the amount of tension used to squeeze the muscle groups.

Practise this routine with all of the muscle groups on the list a couple of times a day until you are able to achieve a profound sensation of physical relaxation.

Second objective: to reduce the time required for relaxation

To do this, instead of working with specific parts of your body, you will have to follow the same tension/relaxation procedure with these four areas:

1. Lower limbs

2. Abdomen and chest

3. Arms, shoulders, and neck

4. Face

Thus, for example, with the 'lower limbs' area concentrate on both legs and feet at the same time.

Perform the contraction/relaxation routine with these areas twice a day until you are able to achieve a good level of relaxation.

Third objective: to relax without the need for prior tension

While you perform the tension/relaxation protocol with the grouped muscle areas concentrate on your breathing. Inhale slowly while you apply and maintain the muscle tension. Afterwards, when you relax them and breathe out, say a cue word or phrase to yourself such as 'relax', 'let it go', 'it's OK', 'warm and heavy', 'soft', 'stay calm', 'I feel in tune' or anything of your choice. After repeating this procedure enough times your brain will associate this cue word or phrase with a state of relaxation. Finally, with practice, the cue word or phrase alone will produce a relaxed state without the need to perform prior tensing.

Whatever the relaxation technique you use, it can be used to achieve what is known as *systematic desensitisation*. In this procedure, events that cause anxiety are recalled in the imagination, and then a relaxation technique is used to dissipate the anxiety. With sufficient repetition through practice, the imagined event loses its anxiety-provoking power. At the end of training, when you actually face the real event, you will find that it too, just like the imagined event, has lost its power to make you anxious.

To relax properly you will find it helpful to take deep breaths. You can do this before a performance as a way of triggering a relaxation response that soothes your body and focuses your mind. Some musicians may also find it helpful to plan a deep breath mid-performance, such as on a long rest, between movements of a piece or rhythmically breathing along with a melodic line.

Deep breathing

Imagine that your lungs are divided into three parts. As you inhale though your nose, the bottom part fills and forces the stomach out (putting your hands on your stomach and rib cage can help you to feel and control this better). Then, expand your thorax, raising the ribs and the chest as the air fills the middle part of the lungs. Finally, fill the top part of the lungs raising the top part of the thorax. Exhale the air through the mouth by pressing the stomach inwards and lowering the thorax to empty the lungs. To maintain a correct breathing rhythm, mentally count to five both as you inhale and exhale. As you control your breathing better you can try to do it for longer counts or by holding your breath between inhaling and exhaling.

Exercising your thinking

Cognitive techniques are based on the assumption that the distortion of a musician's thoughts and beliefs could be the cause of anxiety. They try to identify negative thoughts and replace them with more positive ones. These are the strategies that have been shown to be most effective for musicians.

Seeing anxiety as a positive

This is about identifying negative and irrelevant thoughts about performing and replacing them with optimistic ideas about the task. Before appearing in public a musician is asked to state the symptoms of anxiety that he or she is sure will materialise and helped to reframe them as less threatening, even desirable, reactions. In this way, heart palpitations and more rapid breathing, for example, are reappraised as normal emotional responses that are not conspicuous to an audience and can provide energy, thus contributing to a livelier and more exciting musical performance.

Positive self-talk

This is based on analysing and confronting the veracity of negative and unrealistic thoughts. Anxious musicians are usually prophets of doom about their opportunities to fail. The objective is to help them evaluate their perception about a performance and adopt more positive and helpful statements about themselves, such as 'I'm bound to make a few mistakes, but so does everyone' and 'the audience wants me to play well and will make allowances for a few slips'. This reduces the feeling of being threatened and increases your feeling of self-control.

Mental rehearsal and imagery

Preparation for the performance involves imagining, as vividly as possible, going through the performance in the ideal way you would like it to go. It seems as if this is able to provide a form of neuromuscular programming that makes the musician more capable of behaving automatically in the desired way during the performance (see *Chapter 1 – Basic functions*).

Combined therapies

Since, in the majority of cases, anxiety encompasses elements that are physical (trembling, palpitations, and so forth) and mental (negative or doom-laden thoughts) as well as negative reinforcement (avoidance and escape), the most effective intervention appears to combine different aspects of the techniques mentioned. Progressive exposure, for example, is usually used together with relaxation and mental preparation.

> **Warning:** Some musicians think that because they have had these problems for many years it is too late to correct them as they now form part of their make-up. However, although it is true that it is difficult to change the way you are, it is never too late to change certain specific aspects that allow you to improve and conquer performance anxiety.

Psychological aspects of injury

The mind plays an important role in the opportunities you have to get ill and to get better, and how the symptoms of an injury manifest themselves. It can even make you experience symptoms that are not related to any injury at all.

Imagine, for example, that during a routine check-up for the members of an orchestra the doctor pays special attention to the thumb on the right hand with no real reasons for doing so. With each musician, after checking the thumb very carefully, the doctor says: 'Are you sure that your thumb has never hurt you? Well, if it doesn't bother you, don't worry about it. Actually, there's nothing to worry about. Anyway, if you notice anything strange, come and see me and we'll look at it again.' A large percentage of them will return to the surgery after a few days concerned by the symptoms they have experienced in their hands from then on!

This is because pain or any other symptom is suggestible. On the other hand, it is possible that your physical symptoms are caused by emotional factors, even if you are unaware

difficulties, infections of the respiratory tracts, vomiting, loss of appetite, changes to menstruation, rashes, excessive perspiration, headaches and migraine, disturbed sleep, misty vision and vertigo.

Finally, in the same way that your brain is able to learn and remember a telephone number, a passage of music or the different things that happen during a journey, it is also able to store pain caused by injury in the memory. The more restrictive the injury or the more repercussions it has (psychological, social, employment-related, family, economic, and so forth), the more likely it is to stay engraved in your mind.

This 'remembered pain' can be recalled, return to the consciousness and be felt as if it were real whenever a certain stimulus activates neural circuits where it is stored. As a result, stimulating the area originally affected, concentrating

that you are suffering from an emotional disturbance. These are known as psychosomatic disorders. The most frequent of these are changes in heart rate, fainting, breathing

Creative visualisation

● Sit in a comfortable position and relax.

● Breathe deeply and slowly for a couple of minutes (see page 15).

● When you feel completely relaxed, imagine that you are sitting on the banks of a peaceful river on a spring afternoon with your feet in the water. Put your hands into the water and begin to stir it gently.

● Concentrate on the sensations you feel in your arms and hands. Are they the same on both sides? Do you feel pain or any other symptom?

● Do this for a few minutes.

● When you are able to imagine this situation for several days without experiencing negative sensations in the injured area, practise visualisation when you are performing a more demanding activity such as, for example, watering flowers in the garden, bicycling through the park or typing on your computer keyboard. Once you have gradually mastered these activities you must imagine picking up your instrument. You feel relaxed and happy. You feel no symptoms. You begin to play a scale slowly. Gradually, imagine that you are playing more demanding pieces.

● If any discomfort appears during the visualisation, analyse whether there is tension in any area or any attitude of mind or physical position that may encourage discomfort. Concentrate on this and try to relax the area. Repeat the visualisation on successive days until you manage to perform it without discomfort on several occasions.

too much on feelings or receiving a call inquiring whether you can play in a performance may be sufficient stimuli for you to experience again or aggravate the symptoms associated with an old or recent injury.

Although it cannot be played down and resolving this type of affliction may be complex and require the involvement of a psychologist, creative visualisation could help you to cope with this problem by yourself. This technique has been shown to be effective in avoiding your brain recalling imaginary symptoms of the injury, and more so that certain situations do not cause stage fright.

Quiz

1. Anxiety is:
- a) a desirable and necessary reaction, because it can improve performing results in some musicians;
- b) an exaggerated reaction that can overwhelm some musicians, and can seriously interfere with performance;
- c) both are correct.

2. Performance anxiety:
- a) always manifests as sensation of breathlessness, 'butterflies' in your stomach and palpitations;
- b) rarely produces negative thoughts or leads to irrational decisions;
- c) in some cases could manifest itself exclusively as insomnia, lack of vitality or emotional instability.

3. A good way to improve performance anxiety is:
- a) to take alcohol;
- b) to accept that you have a problem that is not always possible to solve on your own;
- c) to avoid stress-inducing situations.

4. Progressive Muscular Relaxation is:
- a) a way to induce relaxation by deep breathing;
- b) a relaxation technique helpful for dissipating anxiety and muscle tension;
- c) a very difficult technique only useful for musicians experienced in yoga or tai chi.

5. The distortion of musician's thoughts and beliefs:
- a) is rarely the cause of a musician's anxiety;
- b) could be improved by Alexander technique, Progressive Muscular Relaxation or stretching;
- c) in the majority of cases is accompanied by physical symptoms such as trembling and palpitations.

6. It's false that physical symptoms:
- a) could be caused by emotional factors;
- b) could not be improved with psychological work;
- c) could be a stored pain in your memory.

7. Creative visualisation:
- a) could be effective in preventing your brain from recalling the imaginary symptoms of an injury;
- b) is not effective in stage fright;
- c) needs the guidance of a psychologist.

Question	Correct answer	If your answer is wrong, please read the page again and find out why you made your mistake
1	c	see page 80
2	c	see page 81
3	b	see page 82
4	b	see page 85
5	c	see page 87
6	b	see page 87
7	a	see page 88

Chapter 7
Troubleshooting for musicians
Basic body maintenance and solving problems

Maintenance

In the music profession today and in the education and training of professional musicians, things are changing. Until recently it would have been thought laughable to insist that warming-up and cooling-down routines should occupy professional and educational time. However, recent scientific evidence and the shocking statistics coming from the music industry show how vital it is to change years of poor practice both on the rehearsal platform and in the conservatoires and music schools. The routines in this chapter should be common practice throughout the profession and are even more vital in the education process.

To ensure that your body operates well and performs at its best, you should avoid situations that put you at risk (see *Chapter 2 – Situations that place the musician at risk*). You need to learn to protect yourself from poor posture when playing (see *Chapter 3 – Posture*), regularly review your working conditions and routines (see *Chapter 4 – Musicians,*

instruments and the workplace) and perform those physical exercises that will help you to achieve the optimal response and recuperation in order to maintain peak performance. Let's be more specific about these two last points.

General tips

- Don't suddenly increase the time you spend practising or studying (maximum 10-minute increase per day).

- When practising, leave more difficult passages and pieces for towards the middle of the time spent in the studio, when your muscles are warm and not yet tired.

- Increase the speed, difficulty and intensity of your tasks progressively.

- Don't become obsessed with repeating a passage or technical action that you can't quite get right over and over again. So that you don't continuously run along the same worn mental track, look for alternative ways of approaching it.

- When practising, take a 5-minute break every half-hour.

- If your muscles are overloaded, do some stretching.

- Make sure you are working under the best possible conditions (good lighting, noise-free environment, comfortable temperature, regular mealtimes and sleeping habits) (see *Chapter 4 – Musicians, instruments and the workplace*). Avoid playing at the time of day when you are most tired.

- Never play if you are experiencing pain. If you feel any pain, stop playing as soon as you can and do some gentle stretching. If the pain does not go away or if it reappears in subsequent sessions, seek advice from a performing arts specialist.

- Do exercises to stretch your muscles before playing (and whenever you feel like it) and to cool down afterwards.

Your diet should be varied and balanced. Here are some examples of light and healthy meals.

This is an example of what you should eat in a day. The diet must be varied and distributed in 4–5 meals.

1 Eat 2 or 3 pieces of fruit a day as minimum. Natural juices have less fibre than a whole piece of fruit and this is not desirable.

2 An adult musician should drink, at least, two glasses of milk a day. This could be partially substituted by yoghurt or cheese. You should drink whole milk if you are not overweight or do not have high levels of fat in your blood.

3 You could eat up to 3 eggs a week if you do not have high levels of fat in your blood. Hard-boiled eggs or an omelette are good options but, if you are not overweight and you use olive oil, you could eat fried eggs.

4 Pulses (lentils, chickpeas, etc.) should be eaten 2 or 3 times a week. If you eat pulses with cereals (bread, pasta, rice) it is not necessary to eat meat that day.

5 Drink 1–2 litres of water a day, avoiding sweet or alcoholic drinks.

⑥ Doughnuts, croissants or similar pastry products should only be eaten sporadically (once a week and not every day).

⑦ As well as red meat and chicken, eat plenty of both 'white' and 'oily' fish.

⑧ Bread should be wholemeal/grain.

⑨ Sandwiches could be made with tuna, salmon, ham, cheese, etc.

⑩ A good breakfast is important, as you have not had any food for the whole of the night. This should include dairy products (for example, milk, yoghurt or cheese) and cereal (for example, toast or cornflakes). If possible, add a piece of fruit.

⑪ Nuts and raisins must be eaten in moderation if you are overweight; avoid salty varieties if you have hypertension.

⑫ You must eat green vegetables twice a day.

Preparing for peak performance: exercises before and after playing

Before playing

Exercises done before playing are aimed at improving elasticity, warming up muscles, tendons and joints, improving performance, delaying the onset of fatigue and preventing injuries.

The first step is to do a general warm-up away from the instrument that will physically loosen you up. You should start with exercises that work on FLEXIBILITY, and then proceed to the STRETCHES (see page 95).

This should be followed by a specific warm-up that includes a variety of gentle movements on your instrument at a moderate speed and intensity. Strained postures and difficult passages should be avoided. The length of time you need to do this specific warm-up will depend on how much or how hard you intend to practise – 10 to 20 minutes could be enough, but you need a longer warm-up if you intend to play or sing intensively, even if it is only for a short time.

After playing

To help ensure a smooth recovery, it is best not to stop the activity suddenly. An active cool-down stage helps eliminate metabolic waste products, and prevents fatigue and injuries resulting from the cumulative work done.

First, a specific cool-down should be done, gradually reducing the level of activity over a 5-minute period (slower, easier and gentler pieces). Make sure you leave 5 minutes free at the end of your rehearsal period for it.

This should be followed by a general cool-down using the STRETCHES suggested on page 95. Even if you have to hand over the practice room and leave, you can still go through a cool-down routine in the corridor or as you are walking away.

Exercises for flexibility

These are exercises for before playing. Flexibility exercises work on muscle elasticity and tone, joint mobility and coordination.

● They prepare muscles for stretching and for playing.

● They are a good way to move from rest to activity.

● They help prevent injuries.

● They should always be done before playing.

● They can be done whenever you feel that your muscles are tight.

● No special equipment or clothing is needed.

● Breathing should be slow and rhythmically controlled.

● Movements should be slow and gentle, based on a back-and-forth motion, and should not involve straining or cause pain.

● When undertaking these flexibility exercises you should not compare yourself with other musicians.

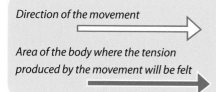

Direction of the movement

Area of the body where the tension produced by the movement will be felt

Neck tilt

Tilt your head slowly from side to side without straining. Avoid raising your shoulders. Repeat 10 times.

Shoulders

Roll both shoulders backwards through a full circle. Repeat 10 times.

Head turns

Turn your head slowly from one shoulder to the other without straining. Never push beyond the point of resistance. Repeat 10 times.

Arms

Bend the elbows and wrists of both arms. Next, extend both arms completely with your wrists bent well back. Repeat 10 times.

Flexibility

93

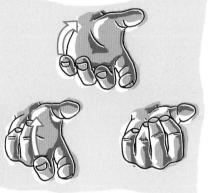

Hand opening and closing

Bend your fingers one by one. When they are all in the bent position, straighten them again one by one. Repeat 10 times.

Finger spread

Slowly spread your fingers as far apart as you can, and then bring them back together. Repeat 10 times.

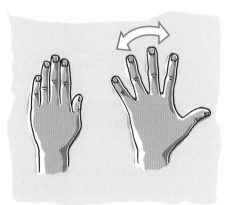

Back twist

Twist your entire back with the help of a swinging motion of your arms, while trying to avoid any twisting of your legs. Your head should remain looking to the front. Repeat 10 times.

Stretches

These are exercises for before and after playing. They are short and simple enough also to use in breaks in playing. Stretches prepare muscles for playing and result in greater tolerance of the effort involved. They help muscles recover after activity and are a good way to prevent injuries.

● No special equipment is required.

● When stretching, you should relax and get comfortable.

● Breathing should be slow, rhythmic and controlled.

● Stretches should not involve bouncing or jerky movements.

● Avoid pain: you should only note a pleasant tension.

● Don't compare yourself to other musicians. Stretching is not a competition. The following figures only show you the direction and the parts of the body involved in each stretch but not the degree of stretching.

● Start with the side where you feel more tension or discomfort (unconsciously you tend to spend longer on the side you start with).

● Stretches should be done both before and after playing.

● It is important to make stretching a regular habit. It is relatively easy to remember to do stretches when you feel discomfort or muscle tension, but easy to forget that they should also be done when you feel recovered or if you have never been injured.

● Stretching can be done anywhere and at any time.

Stretches should be held for 20–30 seconds. Stretch one side, then the other, and repeat if necessary.

Palms

Put the fingertips of your hands together. Press your hands together and try to bring your fingers into contact along their complete length. Don't pull your wrists back, lower your elbows or put the palms of your hands together. Hold this position for 20–30 seconds.

Thumb

Pull the thumb of one hand back using your other hand. Hold this position for 20–30 seconds, and then repeat with the other hand.

Fist

Make a fist with your thumb inside. Take your fist in your other hand and bend it forward at the wrist while straightening your arm. Hold this position for 20–30 seconds, and then repeat with the other arm.

Hand back

Using your other hand, bend your wrist back while keeping your fingers and your arm straight. Hold this position for 20–30 seconds, and then repeat with the other arm.

Lateral

Take hold of one wrist with your other hand and pull it up and to the side. Hold this position for 20–30 seconds, and then repeat with the other arm.

Upper body

Extend your arm back with the palm of your hand against the corner of a piece of furniture or doorframe. Pull forward with your shoulder. Hold this position for 20–30 seconds, and then repeat with the other arm.

Back

Let your upper body fall forward with your arms hanging at the sides of your legs. Arch your back fully from your head down. Hold this position for 20–30 seconds.

Neck

Tilt your head sideways without raising your shoulder. Hold this position for 20–30 seconds, and then repeat on the other side.

Head forward

Starting from the position of the previous stretch and without straightening your neck, tilt your head forward. You should feel the stretch at the back of your neck. Keep your shoulders as low as you can. Hold this position for 20–30 seconds, and then repeat on the other side.

Head back

Starting from the sideways-neck-stretch position and without straightening your neck, let your head fall back. You should feel the stretch on the outside of your neck. Keep your shoulders as low as you can. Hold this position for 20–30 seconds, and then repeat on the other side and gently return to the starting position.

The small arrows on the illustrations indicate the area of the body where the tension produced by the stretch should be felt.

Stretches

Complementary physical activity

As with most daily activities, playing an instrument causes imbalances that you need to correct. You can do this through regular physical activity, which will also enable you to improve your general health, increase your performance and fine tune your emotional response for concerts and performances.

What type of physical activity is most advisable for a musician?

You should choose an activity that is suitable for your physical abilities and limitations. However, it should, above all, be pleasant and achievable. So, for example, the pianist who is overweight and has knee problems should not choose jogging as the impact will cause injury. This pianist should consider swimming, for example. But we wouldn't recommend swimming to a flautist with back or shoulder problems, especially crawl or breaststroke, as these styles place a great demand on precisely these areas.

These two musicians practise sports that are not complementary to their musical activity as they are reproducing the same posture and stress the same areas.

Overloaded zone or type of injury	jogging	skating	walking	cycling	swimming crawl	swimming backstroke	tennis-paddle	golf	cross-country skiing	ballroom dancing
cervical spine (spasm, radiculopathy disc problems or arthritis)	no	yes	yes	no	no	yes	ask	ask	yes	ask
lumbar spine (spasm, sciatica, disc problems or arthritis)	no	ask	ask	ask	no	yes	no	no	ask	ask
shoulder (impingement, bursitis, ruptured tendons)	yes	yes	yes	yes	no	no	no	no	yes	ask
fingers (trigger finger, joint inflammation or pain)	yes	yes	yes	yes	yes	yes	no	no	no	yes
wrist (synovial cyst, de Quervain's tendinitis, carpal tunnel syndrome)	yes	yes	yes	no	yes	yes	no	no	ask	yes
elbow-forearm (muscle overuse, tennis elbow, golfer's elbow, ulnar tunnel syndrome...)	yes	yes	yes	no	yes	yes	no	no	no	yes
knees (meniscus and ligament injuries or articular degeneration)	no	no	ask	ask	yes	yes	ask	ask	ask	ask

You should look for an activity that will be complementary and which doesn't work your body in the same way as when you are playing your instrument. In addition, the activity must work those areas that you don't use when you're playing and must not damage the muscles or joints already overloaded by instrument practice or which are already injured.

Every physical activity tends to work some areas more than others. Choose one that is most suitable to you according to the part of your body that you tend to overload or have injured (see the table on page 97 – the diagnoses that appear between brackets are described on page 105–7 – **yes**: this activity is suitable to your condition, **no**: not recommended, **ask**: depends on the exact diagnosis and exactly how the activity is performed – ask your doctor or performing arts specialist).

Activities that involve the gentle use of the large muscle groups are most suitable. Amongst others these include vigorous walking, trekking, running, rowing, skating, cross-country skiing, swimming, cycling (with raised handlebars to avoid forced posture of the spine), stair-walking, dance or ballroom dancing. As a general concept, those activities aimed to increase muscle volume or that could produce asymmetric muscular growth, such as body-building or asymmetric sports, should not be the basic activity for musicians.

On the other hand, you should avoid or consider very carefully the risks of some sports where there is a possibility of physical contact with fellow participants or objects (football, basketball, volleyball, and so on). You should take into account the risk of impacts to the fingers or face.

How intense should the exercise be?

If your objective in performing the activity is to achieve and maintain a good physical condition, exercising for between 20 and 60 minutes three times a week will be enough. If, in addition, you want to lose weight, you need to plan for five exercise days a week together with monitoring your diet.

In no circumstances should the activity be exhausting.

General tips for complementary activity

1. Choose a pleasant and accessible activity. Consider practising it with other people as this reduces the risk of losing interest.

2. The activity must be suitable to your own characteristics and complementary to your musical practice.

3. Practice must be regular, about three days a week, without large breaks that could set you back.

4. Progressively increase the duration and intensity of the sessions.

5. Remember that you must do a warm-up and a cool-down (this could be similar to what you are doing during your musical practice, see pages 92-96). Do not begin or stop the activity suddenly.

6. Regularly drink water or isotonic beverages before, during and after the activity.

Keep up a good rhythm without straining excessively. A guide to working at the correct level is a raised heart rate and increased breathing, but not shortness of breath.

Solving problems

Table of symptoms

This manual is not a substitute for a correct diagnosis from a doctor or performing arts specialist or a prescription for a suitable treatment. However, it does offer some basic directions that can help you to solve slight complaints and guide you towards the type of action you should take. Whatever the symptom, the first thing to do when a problem appears is to review and correct those factors that could have caused it (see *Chapter 2 – Situations that place the musician at risk*).

Symptom	Probable cause	Corrective action
Pain	● Generally indicates tissue damage, that something is not working properly. ● It is not usually a specific symptom of a complaint and any change in work rhythm or overuse may bring on this warning signal.	● Reduce the work intensity. If this does not reduce the pain, stop playing. ● Stretch the affected area gently (see page 95), avoiding exercises that cause an increase in pain. ● Apply cold if the pain is in your extremities or heat if it is in your back (see page 101).
Fatigue (muscular or vocal)	● Excessive work. ● Lack of rest. ● Technical fault. ● Muscle imbalance. ● General exhaustion. ● Irregularity or sudden changes in the intensity of work.	● Review work routines (see page 3). ● Take more frequent breaks. ● Analyse your technique. ● Evaluate the ergonomic characteristics of the instrument (see page 45). ● Stretch the affected muscles (see page 94). ● Apply cold after playing (see page 101).
Inflammation	● Over-repetition of gestures or passages. ● Working in strained positions. ● General illnesses.	● Reduce the exercise intensity. If this does not reduce the inflammation, stop playing. ● Apply cold (see page 101). ● If there is stiffness, you could apply heat (see page 101). ● Review working postures (see page 26).
Tension in the back (muscle contraction)	● Sustained poor posture. ● Physical or psychological stress. ● Excessive tension when playing or singing. ● Weight of instrument inefficiently supported.	● Review working postures (see page 26). ● Apply heat (see page 101). ● Perform flexibility exercises and stretching (see page 95) of the area affected. ● Analyse whether you can improve the way you hold your instrument (see page 27).
Pins and needles, numbness, change in sensitivity	● Poor posture. ● Excessive pressure from the instrument or other objects on a particular area of your body. ● Inflammation or tension in a particular area.	● Review working postures (see page 26). ● Analyse whether there are areas of excessive contact pressure with the instrument, or backpack strap (see page 41).

Symptom	Probable cause	Corrective action
Lack of agility, lack of control or tension in the hand, neck or mouth area	● Over-repetition of a technical action. ● Sudden change in work intensity or method. ● Physical or psychological stress. ● Poor conflict resolution during the process of learning new material.	● Stop playing. ● Begin playing the passage at the point where the problem appears, lowering your speed until the symptoms disappear. Repeat it for a few minutes a day until it has been consolidated. On subsequent days, increase the speed without reaching the point where any symptoms appear. ● If you are not able to progress because the symptoms reappear, vary the way you perform the passage (accentuate notes, change the rhythm, break up the passage etc.). ● If none of this solves the problem, stop playing and consult a specialist in performing arts medicine.
Sore throat	● Most commonly viral, occasionally bacterial infections (cold, pharyngitis, tonsillitis). ● Gastro-oesophageal reflux.	● Increase your water intake – drink frequently. ● Medical treatment. ● Review dietary habits.
Hoarseness	● Common cold. ● Nodules or haematoma on the vocal folds. ● Allergies.	● Complete vocal rest. ● Increase your water intake – drink frequently. ● Medical treatment but avoid oral antihistamines (frequently given as decongestants).
Impossible to sing high notes	● Muscle strain through overload. ● Stress. ● Anxiety.	● Laryngeal massage. ● Neck stretching exercises. ● Relaxation techniques. ● Review vocal technique. ● Increase your water intake – drink frequently.
Voice cracking	● Insufficient support. ● Injury to vocal folds.	● Review vocal technique. ● Medical investigation. ● Increase your water intake – drink frequently.
Nasal congestion	● Common cold. ● Allergies.	● Increase your water intake – drink frequently. ● Medical treatment.

Tools

A whole arsenal of possible treatments is within your reach. But these treatments are not all effective for every problem – some may even cause you harm. Here you have a description of the most used with some information about their usefulness and precautions.

Cold

Applying cold helps to retard or reduce inflammation and pain by reducing blood flow to the area and numbing the nerve endings. The reduction of pain decreases the extent of secondary muscle tension.

Methods of application: The most practical way is to use ice cubes inside a bag or, even better, cold packs. Packs of small frozen vegetables can make a good and readily available substitute. You can also submerge the hands or feet in iced water. The application time may be five minutes, if a small superficial structure is involved (for example a finger or the lips), or up to 20 minutes if the affected area is deep and large (hip or knee). Cold sprays and creams are not very helpful as they only cool the surface of the skin.

Precautions: You must avoid direct contact between the cold source and the skin, in order to prevent tissue damage from the cold, by placing a cloth between the ice and the skin. Generally, the application of cold during the first 3 minutes produces only a feeling of cold. Between 2 minutes and 7 minutes a burning sensation and slight pain can be felt. If you continue to apply the cold, stiffness and numbness sets

Warning: The application of cold for an excessive period of time or pressing too hard on an area may burn the skin or damage the small nerves that run beneath it. Moreover, there are people who are hypersensitive to cold. So, if you start to itch, have spots on the skin, pain and inflammation you should avoid extreme use of cold.

in. This is the moment when you must remove the ice and not before. Don't use ice to numb an injury in order to play without feeling the pain.

Heat

The application of heat relaxes the tissues, decreases joint stiffness, reduces pain, relieves muscle spasm and increases blood flow. It is particularly helpful for back pain and muscle spasm. In these cases you should stretch the areas after applying the heat.

Methods of application: Hot packs are bags filled with a substance that can be reheated several times. Some types can be reheated in microwaves. You should apply the bags for between 15 and 20 minutes but check the skin every 5 minutes to avoid burns. Another option would be to use a hot-water bottle filled with water from a pre-boiled kettle; theses are applied in the same way as hot packs but transfer less heat. Finally, electric heat pads have the advantage of maintaining their heat for as long as you want, but you risk burning yourself if you fall asleep with them turned on.

Precautions: Do not apply immediately after an injury occurs, nor in areas that are swollen or where there is a skin injury or an open wound.

Contrast baths

Alternating cold and heat increases blood flow.

Methods of application: Although there are different guidelines, the following may be used: submerge your hand or forearm in a container of warm water (34–38ºC) for 3 minutes. Next, place it in iced water (10–15ºC) for 1 minute. Repeat for 20 minutes and always end the session with cold immersion.

Precautions: The same as with cold or heat separately.

Stretching

Although we have included stretching within the warm-up and cool-down protocol, you can perform these exercises at any time to relieve tension and improve mobility (see page 95).

Massage

Massage is the manipulation of muscles and surrounding tissues to improve their function and to promote relaxation and welfare. It is usually used to relieve muscle spasm and tension.

Methods of application: There are many forms of massage and all of them should be administered by a professional therapist guided, where necessary, by a doctor's or physiotherapist's diagnosis. In any event, if the massage is superficial without excessive pressure, you can do it yourself. One option for massaging the back is to use a soft rubber ball about the same size as a tennis ball. You should lie on the floor or lean against a wall with the ball between you and the floor or wall. By changing position and the pressure through your body movements you will give yourself a gentle massage on the overloaded areas.

Precautions: Using massage on some injuries may make them worse. Therefore, if there are any doubts, leave massage to trained hands.

Rest

This means preventing the injured area from being exposed to activities that may aggravate the injury. With the exception of some minor ailments, rest in itself does not usually cure an injury.

Methods of application: The level of rest can be very variable. We talk about relative rest when we avoid only certain activities or the most harmful technical gestures, allowing a certain level of activity. Absolute rest means avoiding all activity. It doesn't make much sense to stop playing completely but then to continue typing at the computer or carrying heavy items. Moreover, to avoid a deterioration in technique as far as possible, whenever you have to take a slightly extended break, it would be a good idea to perform mental practice (see page 13).

Precautions: Prolonged rest causes the loss of physical and, obviously, technical ability. If the problem does not disappear after a maximum of one week's rest, you should consult a doctor.

Strappings and bandages

Joints and muscles can be supported by bandages, orthopaedic tape or detachable splints to reduce their mobility and/or movement and support contraction. Their greatest effect, however, is to remind you to avoid forced movements of the injured area.

Precautions: You should not wear a bandage for too long or too tightly as it may compress and irritate parts of the body such as nerves, blood vessels or sensitive skin.

Immobilisation

This is used in order to impose complete rest on the affected area.

Methods of application: Casts, plaster or plastic may be used on fingers, wrists or elbows. These are usually used following a traumatic injury and you should never use them without a doctor's or performing arts specialist's instruction.

Precautions: Prolonged immobilisation may cause stiffness, especially in the finger joints. Therefore, your doctor or physiotherapist must assess your injury correctly and, taking into account that you are a musician, decide whether there are alternatives to immobilisation and, in any event, restrict its use to the minimum time required.

Progressive criteria

Sudden changes in intensity or type of work are usually poorly tolerated (see *Chapter 2 – Situations that place the musician at risk*). After holidays or following an injury, it is not advisable to resume activity in an abrupt manner.

The table below offers a guide to how to increase your activity gradually, which is designed mainly for musicians who have been injured but which may show you how to increase intensity incrementally in other circumstances.

● Begin the process at the first level (total playing time 10 minutes, divided into 5 minutes of playing initially, a pause for, at least, an hour and 5 more minutes of playing).

● Don't forget to begin and end the session by performing the exercises on page 92–6.

● If you feel some discomfort when playing, stop and apply cold in the affected area for 10 minutes. Abandon the session and, on the following day, start again and play for less time.

● According to how your body responds, you should remain on each level for between 3 and 7 days. If you feel comfortable at that level, you may go on to the next.

● The last minutes of playing each day should be very gentle to allow an active cooling-down period for the muscles.

● In the same way as you should increase practice time gradually, you should also begin playing simpler pieces gently and gradually introduce more demanding techniques and passages as and when your progress allows.

● From the last level onwards you should increase your efforts freely until you reach your normal work pattern. But continue with small breaks every 25–30 minutes and don't make sudden increases in your workload.

Total playing time	p	r	p	r	p	r	P	r	p	r	p	r	p	r	p	r	p	r	p
10'	5'	60'	5'																
15'	8'	60'	7'																
20'	10'	50'	10'																
25'	10'	50'	10'	60'	5'														
35'	15'	40'	15'	60'	5'														
50'	20'	30'	20'	50'	10'														
65'	25'	20'	25'	40'	10'	45'	5'												
1h 30'	25'	15'	25'	30'	25'	40'	10'	10'	5'										
2h 5'	25'	10'	25'	20'	25'	25'	10'	10'	5'	2h	20'	20'	10'	10'	5'				
2h 30'	25'	10'	25'	10'	25'	15'	10'	5'	5'	2h	25'	20'	20'	30'	10'	10'	5'		
2h 55'	25'	10'	25'	10'	25'	10'	10'	5'	5'	3h	25'	15'	25'	30'	20'	30'	10'	10'	5'
3h 20'	25'	5'	25'	5'	25'	5'	20'	5'	5'	3h	25'	10'	25'	20'	25'	20'	20'	10'	5'

Guidelines for gradual reintroduction. Times are expressed in minutes, p=play and r=rest.

Medicines
Analgesics and anti-inflammatories

These are medicines that relieve pain and reduce inflammation. Some medicines such as acetylsalicylic acid (Aspirin®) and ibuprofen perform both functions. But some, such as indomethacin (prescription only), are good anti-inflammatory drugs with little analgesic effect and others, such as paracetamol, act only as painkillers and have no anti-inflammatory action.

You should bear in mind that the analgesic effect may mask the real condition of your complaint. As secondary effects, some of these drugs may cause inflammation of the stomach and alter the way blood clots with an increased risk of bleeding. You can consult a pharmacist for advice about analgesia, but should avoid taking medication offered by friends. If you seem to require regular medication for longer than a week consult a doctor.

Muscle relaxants

The reduction in muscle tension produced by these drugs can be accompanied by a certain degree of sleepiness, loss of mental agility or reduced playing or singing skills, though there are some modern drugs that may reduce these. Side-effects may diminish with subsequent doses, but they may be very problematic for a musician. For this reason, if your doctor prescribes this type of medication, you should never take it for the first time shortly before an important concert or exam, just in case such secondary effects arise and are harmful to your performance.

Cortisone local injection

This usually refers to the injection of cortisone derivates and anaesthetics into an injured area. The powerful anti-inflammatory effects of cortisone can lead to a rapid improvement in some conditions affecting the tendons and joints. It is therefore a tool that is frequently used. However, you should remember that usually it only suppresses inflammation and does not cure the underlying causes. As a general rule, it should never be used for acute injuries and

you should discuss the pros and cons, including side effects, of such treatment with your doctor. These side effects include, amongst others, the weakening and tearing of tendons and, more rarely, infections. It is therefore advisable to avoid intense activity, especially carrying heavy items, for 10–15 days after the injection.

Betablockers

These are medicines that temporarily reduce the symptoms of anxiety. They are used very frequently by musicians, too often without professional medical advice. Sometimes they are only used on 'special occasions' such as exams or important concerts. However, these medicines do not solve anxiety problems and they only provide temporary relief. Some musicians take them habitually without tackling the underlying reasons for their anxiety. They are very safe drugs but are potentially dangerous in those who suffer from asthma or chronic lung disease, and they can cause significant imbalances in individuals with certain illnesses. Moreover, not all musicians need the same dose or to take them as far in advance. For these reasons it is essential that your doctor evaluates whether there are any contraindications to their use in your case. Also, before you use the drug for an important performance, you should test it at a less crucial time to ensure that there are no secondary effects, to adjust the dose, and to ascertain the correct time to take it. For further advice about how to cope with performance anxiety please refer to *Chapter 6 – Mind and music.*

Alcohol

In the initial phase after ingestion and in small quantities, alcohol causes relaxation. This is one of the reasons why some musicians take it before a concert. But, with the passage of time, it is necessary to drink greater amounts to achieve the same effect. This may lead to habituation and damage to various organs in the body. You should therefore not use alcohol as a means of relaxing. In addition, even at low doses, it affects coordination, memory and nerve response, all of which are highly undesirable effects for performers.

Table of diagnoses

As a guideline, we offer a short description below of the complaints that most frequently affect musicians, and their main symptoms and causes.

Diagnosis	Symptom	Cause
Trigger finger	Pain in the base of the finger or palm of the hand that gets worse when the finger is moved. The pain may also be in the back of the finger or hand. In more advanced phases it may make it difficult to move the affected finger, or even block its movement completely.	The tendons that flex the fingers run through fibrous tunnels (see page 67). The rubbing caused by repetitive movements and strained positions thickens the tendon and inflames the surrounding tissues, which prevent it from sliding easily. This makes it difficult for the tendon to slide through the tunnel and may lead to it becoming stuck (creating a feeling of being coiled like a spring).
Overuse of muscles (forearms and mouth)	Tension, fatigue and progressive pain in the forearms or mouth that restrict the ability to perform after playing for a certain time. When affecting the forearm, it is often confused with golfer's or tennis elbow.	This is to do with the gradual poor adaptation of muscles to the type of work for which, during years, you use your hands, arms or mouth. A lack of breaks in your work routine, sudden changes and excessive tension are factors that may lead to its development. It can cause inflammation in the muscles and reduce their performance.
DeQuervain's tendonitis	Discomfort along the back of the thumb and the wrist. In some cases, information or reddening may appear in the area.	Inflammation of the tendons of the thumb on the back of the wrist, in the area where the tendons pass inside narrow channels (see page 67). Repetitive movements of the thumb or sustained efforts in strained postures increase the rubbing of the tendons at this point.
Carpal tunnel syndrome	Numbness, tingling, night pain, reduced feeling, dexterity and strength in the thumb, index finger, middle finger and occasionally the ring finger due to compression of the median nerve (see page 70) at the wrist.	Although there are predisposing hormonal and anatomical factors, the principal causes in the musician are an incorrect wrist position or inflammation of the tendons connected to the fingers.
Ulnar tunnel (Guyon tunnel) syndrome	Discomfort on the inside of the elbow, forearm and hand; numbness, tingling, night pain, reduced feeling and strength in the little finger and ring finger due to compression of the ulnar nerve (see anatomy on page 67) at the elbow or, more rarely, wrist.	Repetition of movements and strained postures of the wrist and elbow may irritate the ulnar nerve. As this nerve goes through the muscles of the forearm, it is not unusual for it to suffer from secondary irritation when inflamed (especially by overuse of the muscles).
Epicondilitis (tennis elbow)/ Epitrocleitis (golfer's elbow)	Tenderness, pain and swelling of the lateral (epicondyle) or medial area (epitroclea) of the elbow, which may extend down towards the forearm and which is aggravated by holding an instrument or objects with the hand. It is not a common condition for a musician.	A good proportion of the muscles of the forearm adhere to the elbow bone (see page 66). Repetitive traction, especially during manual activities that apply impacts (for example, percussion or, in particular, sports or daily activities), inflames and modifies the tissue that connects the muscle to the bone, making the tissue weaker and more prone to irritation.

Diagnosis	Symptom	Cause
Focal dystonia	Difficulty, slowness and/or loss of control over movements or tension in the fingers, arm, larynx or mouth area, which, at least at the beginning, only appears during certain demanding technical actions or passages and not in others or when away from the instrument. You can find more information at www.fcart.org/distonia and www.dystoniafoundation.com	Repeated practice habitually leads to learning or improving a technical action. However, for reasons that are not yet completely understood, these changes can lead to undesired responses. Amongst the precipitating or predisposing causes and factors are intensive practice, sudden changes in some aspect of performance (technical, hours of work, instrument, repertoire, etc.) or psychological stress. Once the first symptoms of dystonia have appeared, the repetition of the technical action concerned will consolidate this inappropriate motor response in the brain, which will then add compensatory new movements.
Back and neck injuries (spasm, impingement, radiculopathy, sciatica, protruded and herniated disc)	Pain, tension or stiffness in the neck or back. May be accompanied by restricted movement and, if the nerves are affected, numbness, pain, or tingling in the arm or leg.	Asymmetrical or continuous postures, tension, muscle imbalances, poor design of the instrument or work environment and incorrect load distribution can cause excessive tension and imbalances in the muscles supporting the spinal column (see 68). The muscle tension itself may be painful (spasm) but, in addition, its associated mechanical changes can lead to inflammation or irritation of some parts of the spine (compression), the nerves which pass through it (radiculopathy or sciatica) or, more rarely a disc injury (protruded or herniated disc) (see page 69).
Irritation of the brachial plexus, thoracic outlet syndrome	Pain, pins and needles, sensation of heaviness, alteration in sensitivity or weakness affecting the shoulders, arm and elbow, which may extend to the hand.	The collection of nerves that leaves the spinal column at neck level (see page 68) runs between bones and muscles. The degeneration of these bones or vertebral discs – but principally pressure on the neck or shoulder (for example from a violin, viola, accordion straps or carrying-case straps) and excessive tension of the neck muscles – can compress and irritate the nerves.
Hypermobility/ hyperlaxity	Mobility of one or several joints beyond their normal range. Although it is usually completely symptom-free, it may make it difficult to hold or use the instrument correctly. It plays a part in overloading the muscles, tendons and ligaments of the affected area causing discomfort in some cases.	It is usually a constitutional or even hereditary condition that causes greater elasticity or less stiffness in the tissues supporting one or more joints.
Shoulder, rotator cuff or subacromial bursitis and tendinitis, impingement syndrome	Pain in the shoulder and/or outer edge of the arm, especially when moving the arm outwards and upwards.	Although it may be caused by a fall, it is usually due to muscle imbalances and repetitive arm-raising movements that rub the tendons. These lead to inflammation, calcification, fraying or rupture of the tendons that raise the arm (see page 67).

Diagnosis	Symptom	Cause
Ganglion or synovial cyst	Bump or mass that forms under the skin, most commonly on the back of the wrist or the fingers. It may be painful when subjected to pressure or during full-range movements of the affected area, thereby limiting them.	A fluid-filled sac formed when tissues surrounding certain joints or tendons become inflamed and swell up with lubricating fluid. They can increase in size when the tissue is irritated with repetitive movements or bad postures. They often can 'disappear' spontaneously and may be rock-hard due to the high pressure of the mucous-like fluid contained within the cyst.
Rupture of the orbicular muscle of the lips	Sudden pain in part of a wind instrumentalist's lips during a performance. It may be accompanied by some degree of inflammation.	The face muscles are extremely slender. Excessive tension may rupture one of the fibres causing pain, inflammation and intramuscular bleeding. If it does not heal correctly, it can leave a muscle scar that restricts the correct action of the muscle.
Temporo-mandibular joint dysfunction	Alteration and/or inflammation of the joint that links the jaw with the head just in front of the ear. There may be clicking in the area.	Its causes include jaw-clenching and teeth-grinding, which accompany psychological stress and physical pressure, and repetitive and asymmetric movements of the jaw (e.g. in singers, wind or string instrumentalists).
Acute laryngitis	Dry cough, sore or tickly throat, hoarseness, difficulty in swallowing, and a continual need to clear the voice.	Refers to an inflammation of the mucous membrane generally due to a virus. It may be caused by overusing the voice, irritants (smoke, dust, etc.) or exposure to extreme temperatures.
Nodules on the vocal folds	Although some nodules do not result in any symptoms, they usually cause hoarseness, breathiness, loss of range and vocal fatigue.	A thickening of the tissue covering the vocal folds (the mucous membrane) on the point of maximum impact for phonation that is caused more by speaking and singing.
Haematoma of the vocal folds	Sudden pain and disphony, which prevents vocal activity from continuing.	Rupture of venous capillaries with blood spilling on to the vocal folds due to excessive vocal effort. May be encouraged by infections, hormonal changes (e.g. menstrual cycle) and using aspirin.
Laryngitis from gastro-oesophageal reflux	Fluctuating hoarseness during the day, clearing one's throat, pain or sensation of a foreign body in the throat. Although digestive symptoms are frequently not present, there may also be burning at the entrance to the stomach or regurgitation of acid.	Inflammation of the larynx due to acid rising from the stomach to the pharynx.
Stage fright	Fear of not giving a good performance, making mistakes or suffering memory lapses. Accompanied by physical symptoms such as restlessness, gastro-intestinal changes, excessive sweating, cold skin, accelerating heart rate and breathing difficulties.	Your education, social pressure – usually incorporating irrational perfectionism – and even genetic predisposition introduce the possibility of 'failure' when performing. This leads to a disproportionate physical reaction from your brain that can take many forms.

Note: The common term 'RSI' (repetitive strain injury) is much in use, but is not considered particularly useful in this context, as it refers to a multitude of different conditions with different causes and remedies (trigger finger, muscle overuse, tenosinovitis, etc.).

> **Warning:** Tendonitis is often diagnosed, even by some doctors, based on symptoms that are not always to do with inflammation of a tendon. Thus, for example, it is not unusual for a musician to be given this diagnosis when suffering from pain in the upper or middle part of the forearm where, as you can see on page 66, there are no tendons. In any case, the treatment should be based on diagnosis of the condition and not only on symptoms with this kind of popular label.

Quiz

1. As general tips you should:

a) leave more difficult passages and pieces for the end of the rehearsal period;

b) repeat a wrong passage as many times as possible to ensure correction;

c) take 5-minute breaks every half-hour.

2. If you are experiencing pain when you play, you should:

a) continue playing and, if it reappears in subsequent sessions, do some gentle stretching;

b) stop playing as soon as possible and do some gentle stretching;

c) take pain-killers and do some gentle stretching.

3. Exercises done before playing can:

a) reduce your performance endurance if you are not an athlete;

b) improve performance, delay the onset of fatigue and prevent injuries;

c) interfere with muscle memory.

4. Specific warm-up:

a) includes a variety of gentle movements on your instrument at a moderate speed and intensity without strained postures or difficult passages;

b) is not necessary if you are going to have a long and hard rehearsal;

c) the two previous sentences are correct.

5. To facilitate a smooth recovery after playing:

a) stop suddenly and perform flexibility exercises for the last 5 minutes;

b) gradually reduce the level of activity (less speed, difficulty and intensity) for the last 5 minutes;

c) use flexibility and stretching exercises if you experience pain or fatigue during the last 5 minutes.

6. Flexibility exercises are:

a) only for before playing;

b) useful for injury prevention but will not prepare you to play;

c) slow and gentle movements that should not cause pain.

7. Stretches are exercises for before and after playing that:

a) bounce joints and could cause muscle pain;

b) must be performed only when you are injured;

c) prepare muscles for playing and help to recover after activity.

8. Complementary physical activity is carried out to:

a) increase muscle mass;

b) correct imbalances created by playing and daily activities;

c) substitute stretching.

9. The sentence 'complementary physical activity will enable you to improve general health, music performance and emotional response' is:

   a) true;

   b) true, but only if you do a suitable activity for you;

   c) true, but only if you do it in a gym and have a personal trainer.

10. Which of the following physical activities is probably not advisable for a musician:

    a) body-building;

    b) vigorous walking;

    c) ballroom dancing.

11. Which is a good routine for complementary physical activity:

    a) 20 to 60 minutes three times a week, if your objective is to maintain a good physical condition;

    b) 20 to 60 minutes three times a week plus diet monitoring, if your objective is also weight reduction;

    c) both are correct.

12. When do you need to see a doctor?

    a) Never, if you have completely understood this manual.

    b) You should consult a performance arts specialist immediately after the first symptom of discomfort or pain.

    c) If the symptoms appear every time you play, get worse or do not improve with the general tools and counselling included in this manual.

13. It's false that:

    a) rest, by itself, will rarely resolve musicians' problems completely;

    b) cold is particularly useful for back pain and muscle spasm;

    c) it is important to resume your work schedule gradually after an injury or your holidays.

14. Injection of cortisone into an injured area:

    a) is always helpful for musicians;

    b) is especially useful for acute injuries as it normally also cures the underlying causes;

    c) could damage tendons.

Question	Correct answer	If your answer is wrong, please read the page again and find out why you made your mistake
1	c	see page 2
2	b	see page 3
3	b	see page 3
4	a	see page 92
5	b	see page 92
6	c	see page 92
7	c	see page 94
8	b	see page 97
9	b	see page 97
10	a	see page 98
11	a	see page 98
12	c	see page 101
13	b	see page 101
14	c	see page 104

About this book

Jaume Rosset i Llobet

Author Dr Rosset graduated in Medicine and Surgery at the Universitat Autònoma de Barcelona and as Doctor of Medicine and Surgery at the Universitat de Barcelona. He is a specialist in Sports Medicine and also a specialist in Orthopaedic Surgery. He has a postgraduate qualification in Scientific Communication and was collaborator of the medical supplements of *La Vanguardia*. He began his work in arts medicine at the beginning of the 1990s in the Hospital General de Manresa (Barcelona) where he founded a Medical-Surgical Arts Medicine Unit sharing its direction until the year 2001. He was founder and is presenty medical director of the Institut de Fisiologia i Medicina de l'Art-Terrassa and Director of the Fundació Ciència i Art and Co-Director of the Konstanz-Terrassa Dystonia Programme. He is author of several scientific works, collaborates with several musical magazines and participates in the diffusion of information on preventative aspects for artists.

Institut de Fisiologia i Medicina de l'Art-Terrassa (Institute of Physiology and Medicine of Art – Terrassa)

After ten years of experience in the Hospital General de Manresa (Barcelona), the members of the Medical-Surgical Arts Medicine Unit of this centre tried to realise an ambitious project: to bring together different health professionals with experience in the treatment of performing artists in a purpose-built infrastructure and with equipment suited to their needs. Their main objective continues to be able to offer a complete and specialized service for musicians, dancers, singers and actors. Since its inception, the Institute has been at the forefront of research work that has already placed it in the vanguard of arts medicine (www.institutart. com).

George Odam

Head of Research and Staff Development at the Guildhall School of Music & Drama, London, Co-author George Odam is also Emeritus Professor of Music Education at Bath Spa University from 1999. He is a composer, writer and lecturer with interests across the arts. A composition student of Alexander Goehr, he also studied with Jonathan Harvey and Hans Keller and his works for young performers have been played throughout the UK in Europe and Australia. Principal co-author of *Silver Burdett Music 1-4: British Edition* (Stanley Thornes, 1989), his book on music education in practice *The Sounding Symbol* (Nelson Thornes 1995) has been widely acclaimed and he is editor of the new Guildhall Research Studies series with Ashgate Publishing including *Seeking the Soul: The Music of Alfred Schnittke* (2002), Graham Johnson's *Britten: Voice & Piano* (2003) and, with Dr Nicholas Bannan, *The Reflective Conservatoire* (2005).

Àxel Oliveres i Gili

All the illustrations for this book are by Àxel Oliveres, who was born in Terrassa, Catalonia, Spain, but soon moved to a very small village where he grew up almost alone. There he felt that time had stopped and there also he met his best friends: stones, shooting stars, insects, mysterious nature sounds, clouds, lizards, some free abnormals who were social outcasts, solitude and a healthy poverty.

As an adult he moved to the big town. There he studied to become a doctor, but was equally fascinated by other fields such as astronomy and astrophysics, biology, palaeontology, geology, zoology and botany, art history, quantum theory, relativity, topology, epistemology and mind theory. He worked in radio, TV, advertising agencies, drug laboratories and scientific press, as a speaker, scriptwriter, writer and illustrator. But because he was still in love with his old friends, he changed his career and became an artist.

Tragically, Àxel was killed in a road accident in late autumn 2006, during the last stages of preparation of this book.

The book was designed by John Peacock and the copy editor was Sara Peacock.

Where you can find more information and medical assistance

Finland

Finnish Society for Musician's Medicine

hvastama@paju.oulu.fi

France

Médecine des Arts
715 Chemin du Quart
F - 82 000 MONTAUBAN
Phone : +33(0)5 63 20 08 09

mda@medecine-des-arts.com
www.medecina-des-arts.com

Germany

Deutsche Gesellschaft für Musikphysiologie und
Musikermedizin
Kurzes Land 1
32549 Bad Oeynhausen
Tel.: 05731 538933
Fax: 05731 538944

schuppert@dgfmm.org
www.dgfmm.org

Arts Medicine Europe
Belfortsrasse 5
D-81667 Munich
Germany
Tel +49 (0)89 6885200
Fax +49 (0)89 6885907

ame@arts-medicine-europe.org
www.arts-medicine-europe.org

New Zealand

Arts Medicine Aotearoa New Zealand
PO Box 17 215, Karori, Wellington

www.converge.org.nz/amanz/

Switzerland

Schweixerische Gesellschaft Musik-Medizin/Swiss Music
Medicine Association
Haus Tromboasis
Rumiweg 4
CH 4539 Farnem
Tel. +41 (0) 326361771
Fax. +41 (0) 326361725

www.musik-medizin.ch
info@musik-medizin.ch

The Netherlands

Nederlandse Vereniging voor Dans- en
MuziekGeneeskunde
Postbus 432
2501 CK Den Haag

www.nvdmg.nl
info@nvdmg.nl

United Kingdom

British Association of Performing Arts Medicine
4th Floor
Totara Park House
34–36 Grays Inn Road
WC1X 8HR
Helpline:
London:
+44 (0)20 7404 8444
Elsewhere:
+44 (0)845 602 0235

USA

Performing Arts Medicine Association
PO Box 61228
Denver, CO 80206
Tel and Fax: 303-632-9255

artsmed@comcast.net
www.artsmed.org

You can also contact the national members of the *International Musicians' Medicine Committee* to seek for more information

Australia

Bruce Barber	bruce@nari.mednwh.unimelb.edu.au
John Bradshaw	john.l.bradshaw@sci.monach.edu.au
Darryl Coote	Darryl.Coote@arts.monash.edu.au
Vanessa Lim	v.lim3@pgrad.unimelb.edu.au

Austria

Roland Beisteiner	a5381mae@univie.ac.at

Canada

Bonnie Robson	wicked@reach.net
Christine Zaza	zaza@uwo.ca

Czech Republic

Frantisek Sram	SramFr@mbox.vol.cz

Finland

Miikka Peltoma	miikka.peltomaa@iki.fi
Martti Vastamaki	martti.vastamaki@invalidisaatio.fi

France

André-Francois Arcier	mda@worldnet.fr

Germany

Eckart Altenmüller	altenmueller@hmt-hannover.de
Jochen Blum	blummainz@t-online.de
Heide Goertz	hgoertz@mail.hdk-berlin.de
Helmut Möller	moeller@asfh-berlin.de
Maria Schuppert	dgfmm-schuppert@gmx.de

Greece

Theodore Cavour	tcavour23@hotmail.com

Italy

Massimo Ceruso	ceruso@dada.it

The Netherlands

Rob Nolet	rnolet@myotech.nl
Boni Rietveld	MCDM@mchaaglanden.nl

Spain

Jaume Rosset	26920jrl@comb.es

Sweden

Maria Sandgren	Maria.Sandgren@psyk.uu.se

Switzerland

Jörg Kesselring	kesselring.klival@spin.ch

United Kingdom

Robert Butler	rsbutler@aol.com
Rodney Grahame	rodneygrahame@cs.com
Justin Howse	justinhowse@aol.com
Angelina Spurrier	angelina@bpamt.fsnet.co.uk

USA

Alice Brandfonbrener	agbmppa@northwestern.edu
William Dawson	w-dawson@northwestern.edu
Richard Hoppman	hoppmann@RICHMED.MEDPARK.SC.EDU
Mitchell Kahn	drmitchellkahn@pol.net
Frederic Langendorf	lange002@tc.umn.edu
Richard Lederman	LEDERMR@ccf.org
Ralph Manchester	rmanchester@uhs.rochester.edu

Recommended bibliography

You can find further information about your body functioning and maintenance in the following works. Parts of the present manual are based on some of the following publications.

Alcantara, P. (1997) *Indirect Procedures: A Musician's Guide to the Alexander Technique.* Oxford, Great Britain: Clarendon Press.

Andrews, E. (1997) *Healthy Practice for Musicians.* London, Great Britain: Rhinegold Publishing.

Bunch, M.A. (1998) *A Handbook of the Singing Voice.* London, Great Britain: Meribeth Bunch.

Chamagne, P. (1996) *Prévention des troubles fonctionnels chez les musicians.* Onet-le-Château, France: Alexitère.

Chasin, M. (1996) *Musicians and the Prevention of Hearing Loss.* San Diego, USA: Singular Publisher Group.

Conable, B. (1998) *What Every Musician Needs to Know About the Body: The Practical Application of Body Mapping to Making Music.* Portland, USA: Andover Press.

Culf, N. (1998) *Musicians' Injuries. Guide to their Understanding and Prevention.* Guildford, Great Britain: Parapress.

Dalia, G. (2002) *Cómo superar la ansiedad escénica en músicos.* Madrid, Spain: Mundimúsica.

Feldenkrais, M. (1985) *The Potent Self.* New York, USA: Harper & Row.

Gallagher, S.P. and Kryzanowska, R. (1999) *The Pilates Method of Body Conditioning.* Philadelphia, USA: Bain Bridge Books.

Gawler, I. (1997) *The Creative Power of Imagery.* Melbourne, Australia: Hill of Content.

Greene, D. (2002) *Performance Success: Performing your Best under Pressure.* New York, USA: Routledge.

Horvath, J. (2002) *Playing (Less) Hurt.* Kearney, USA: Morris Publishing.

Klein-Vogelbach, S. Lahme, A. and Spirgi-Gantert, I. (2000), *Musikinstrument und Körperhaltung.* Berlin, Germany: Springer.

Klöppel, R. (2003) *Mentales Training für Musiker.* Germany: Gustav Bosse Verlag, Kassel. (There is also a Spanish translation available: *Ejercitación mental para músicos.* Idea Books, 2005.)

Mark, T. (2003) *What Every Pianist Needs to Know about the Body.* Chicago, USA: GIA Publications Inc.

Norris, R. (1993) *The Musician's Survival Manual: A Guide to Preventing and Treating Injuries in Instrumentalists.* Saint Louis, USA: MMB Music.

Orozco, L. and Solé J. (1996) *Tecnopatías del Músico.* Barcelona, Spain: Aritza.

Parncutt, R. and McPherson, G. (ed.) (2002) *The Science and Psychology of Music Performance.* New York, USA: Oxford University Press.

Paull, B. and Harrison, C. (1997) *The Athletic Musician. A Guide to Playing Without Pain.* Lanham, USA: Scarecrow Press.

Peretz, I. and Zatorre, R. (2003) *The Cognitive Neuroscience of Music.* New York, USA: Oxford University Press.

Rosset, J. and Fàbregas, S. (2005) *A tono. Ejercicios para mejorar el rendimiento del músico.* Barcelona, Spain: Paidotribo.

Sardà, E. (2003) *En forma: ejercicios para músicos.* Barcelona, Spain. Paidós.

Sataloff, R. (1998) *Vocal Health and Pedagogy.* San Diego, USA: Singular Publishing Group.

Tortora, G.J. and Derrickson, B.H. (2006) *Introduction to the Human Body: The Essentials of Anatomy and Physiology.* Indianapolis, USA: Wiley.

Wilson, P. (1997) *The Singer's Voice: An Owner's Manual.* Sydney, Australia: Currency Press Inc.

Winspur, I. and Wynn Parry, C.B. (1988) *The Musician's Hand. A Clinical Guide.* London, Great Britain: Martin Dunitz.

Index